ENCYCLOPAEDIA OF EMINENT THINKERS

VOLUME-XIV: **TEJ BAHADUR SAPRU**

Volumes by the same author

The Political Thought of ***Dadabhai Naoroji***
The Political Thought of ***Tej Bahadur Sapru***
The Political Thought of ***C. Rajagopalachari***
The Political Thought of ***Subhas Chandra Bose***
The Political Thought of ***Bhagat Singh***
The Political Thought of ***Annie Besant***
The Political Thought of ***C.R. Das***
The Political Thought of ***Lalalajpat Rai***
The Political Thought of ***Sir Pherozeshah Mehta***
The Political Thought of ***Mahadev Govind Ranade***

About the Author

Dr. (Miss) Ashu Pasricha is a faculty in Gandhian studies at Panjab University, Chandigarh. She has many books to her credit including *Gandhian Approach to Integrated Rural Development; Public Administration: Discipline and Dimensions; Peace Studies: Discipline and Dimensions; WTO, Self-reliance and Globalisation; and Gandhi's Concept of State and Power.* Also, she has published a number of research papers in various Indian and foreign journals of repute.

ENCYCLOPAEDIA OF EMINENT THINKERS

VOLUME FOURTEEN

POLITICAL THOUGHT OF TEJ BAHADUR SAPRU

Dr. Ashu Pasricha
Department of Gandhian Studies
Panjab University, Chandigarh

CONCEPT PUBLISHING COMPANY, NEW DELHI-110 059

Cataloging in Publication Data—DK
Courtesy: D.K. Agencies (P) Ltd. <docinfo@dkagencies.com>

Encyclopaedia of eminent thinkers / K.S. Bharathi.
v. 11-15 ; cm. — (Gandhian studies and peace research series ; 11)
Vols. 11, 14-15 by Ashu Pasricha; v. 12-13 by Jai Narain Sharma.
Includes bibliographical references.
Includes indexes.
ISBN 13: 9788170226840 (set)
ISBN 10: 8170226848 (set)

1. Statesmen—India. 2. Political science—India. 3. India—Politics and government. I. Bharathi, K. S. (Kuduva Swamy), 1956- II. Pasricha, Ashu, 1967- III. Sharma, Jai Narain, 1951- IV. Series: Gandhian studies and peace research series ; 11.

DDC 954.035 22

ISBN-13: 978-81-7022-684-0 (Series)
ISBN-10: 81-7022-684-8 (Series)
ISBN-13: 978-81-8069-494-3 (Vol. XIV)
ISBN-10: 81-8069-494-1 (Vol. XIV)

First Published 2008

Published and Printed by
Ashok Kumar Mittal
Concept Publishing Company
A/15-16, Commercial Block, Mohan Garden
New Delhi-110059 (India)
Phones: 25351460, 25351794
Fax: 091-11-25357103
E-mail: publishing@conceptpub.com

DEDICATED
TO
SUDHIR, SANGEETA
and
SHAWN VERMA

PREFACE

Amongst notable persons that flitted upon the Indian scene, between First World War and India's independence, Dr. Sapru, was one of the most notable. As an advocate, as a constitutional lawyer, as a statesman and as a social reformer, he touched many things and whatever he touched, he touched to adorn it.

In India's struggle for independence against British rule, he acted as a mediatory force between Indian Nationalism and British diehardism. During successive stages of India's march to freedom, from dependency to dyarchy, and from dyarchy to partial autonomy, and from partial autonomy to complete Independence, he unstintedly devoted his great talents and his personal fortune, in influencing British Liberal opinion in favour of India. India even after gaining independence remained within the British Commonwealth, by its own free choice, and this is atributed to Dr. Sapru's contribution which is unique and second to none.

Dr. Sapru was nurtured and educated in the last part of the 19th century. His ideals and values were the ideals and values of his generation, in his case ennobled and exalted by a highly cultured intellect and a strong aesthetic and moral sense. He was genteel distressed by the social evils prevalent in Hindu Society of his days, particularly by the defeatist mentality of the proverbially mild gentoo. He did everything in his power, by his personal example to raise the status of Hindus and of Indians, both in India and abroad.

Dr. Sapru had an intense aversion to the public manifestations of his personality. The material on him largely remained unpublished. I have been prompted by the painful fact that no major publication on Sapru exists. As the first step in the direction of filling a conspicuous lacuna of authentic material about a man, who gave to India, as Harold J. Laski said, "his great gifts of mind and heart," and whose career was "an example to civilization," mine is a humble attempt.

Personal acknowledgments are no easy matters where so many have been kind. My special thanks are due to Professor R. N. Pal, Professor N. Radhakrishnan, Dr. K.S. Bharathi, Dr. A.D. Mishra, Professor Jai Narain Sharma, Dr. Meena Dutta, Dr. Seema Pasricha, Dr. Rashmi Sharma, Dr. Ajit Atri, Ms. Geetanjali Sahni, Mr. Ajay Pasricha (Advocate) and Master Hemant Malhotra. Beyond that I can make only an all embracing salute to the galaxy of the scholars whose works I have consulted.

I am also grateful to Shri Ashok Kumar Mittal, my publisher, for his consistent zeal in the printing and publication of this volume.

Chandigarh **ASHU PASRICHA**

CONTENTS

Encyclopaedia of Eminent Thinkers Series

Vol. I. The Political Thought of **Mahatma Gandhi**/ *K.S. Bharti*
Vol. II. The Political Thought of **Nehru**/ *K.S. Bharti*
Vol. III. The Political Thought of **Rabindra Nath Tagore**/ *K.S. Bharti*
Vol. IV. The Political Thought of **Radhakrishnan**/ *K.S. Bharti*
Vol. V. The Political Thought of **Vinoba**/ *K.S. Bharti*
Vol. VI. The Political Thought of **Aurobindo**/ *K.S. Bharti*
Vol. VII. The Political Thought of **Jayaprakash Narayan**/ *K.S. Bharti*
Vol. VIII. The Political Thought of **Vivekananda**/ *K.S. Bharti*
Vol. IX. The Political Thought of **Ambedkar**/ *K.S. Bharti*
Vol. X. The Political Thought of **M.N. Roy**/ *K.S. Bharti*
Vol. XI. The Political Thought of **Dadabhai Naoroji**/ *Ashu Pasricha*
Vol. XII. The Political Thought of **Veer Savarkar**/ *Jai Narain Sharma*
Vol. XIII. The Political Thought of **M.A. Jinnah**/ *Jai Narain Sharma*
Vol. XIV. The Political Thought of **Tej Bahadur Sapru**/ *Ashu Pasricha*
Vol. XV. The Political Thought of **C. Rajagopalachari**/ *Ashu Pasricha*
Vol. XVI. The Political Thought of **Subhas Chandra Bose**/ *Ashu Pasricha*
Vol. XVII. The Political Thought of **Mohammad Iqbal**/ *Jai Narain Sharma*
Vol. XVIII. The Political Thought of **K.B. Hedgewar**/ *Jai Narain Sharma*
Vol. XIX. The Political Thought of **Bhagat Singh**/ *Ashu Pasricha*
Vol. XX. The Political Thought of **M.S. Golwalkar**/ *Jai Narain Sharma*

1

LIFE AND ACTIVITIES

Tej Bahadur Sapru was born at Aligarh on December 8, 1875. That day marked the beginning of a life story which was destined to assume epic proportions in the fullness of time. It was a period of far-reaching political significance. Less than two decades before his birth, the Great Uprising of 1857 had taken place leading to a complete change in the country's political profile. In 1858 Queen Victoria assumed the title of the Empress of India, marking the heyday of British imperialism in this country. Tej Bahadur's eventful life spanned over more than half a century period, from the final consolidation of that imperialism to its ultimate liquidation, to which his personal contribution was not little.

Tej Bahadur belonged to a highly respectable Kashmiri Pandit family who migrated to Delhi towards the end of the 18th century. The Kashmiri migration flowed to Delhi from where the families got bifurcated, some moving eastwards to U.P., Bihar and Bengal and others proceeding to Central India and Rajasthan. Tej Bahadur's ancestors too migrated likewise, first settling down in Delhi and then moving on to U.P.

Tej Bahadur's grandfather, Pandit Radha Kishan, was a remarkable man. Having received English education in those early days of the British rule, he joined the Delhi College as a teacher of Mathematics and later changed over to government service. He held the post of Deputy Collector with distinction in the Provinces now known as Uttar Pradesh, retiring in the nineties of the last century as the Superintendent of the Doons, quite a big post for an Indian those days. He had a family of seven daughters and one son.

Tej Bahadur's father, Ambika Prasad, was however a different type of a person. A man of much wit and humour, he was by temperament a zamindar and looked after the family estate. But he was also a very generous person. The only son of his father, he too had an only son, Tej Bahadur, and a daughter. No two persons could be more unlike each other than the father and the son. Tej Bahadur, was of an intellectual bent of mind and shared in the progressive trends of the new age. However, he showed great respect for his father, although he had no temperamental affinity with the latter.

When Tej Bahadur was born at Aligarh, his grandfather was posted there as Deputy Collector. Young Tej showed extraordinary talent early enough in his life. The grandfather too was deeply impressed by the promise shown by his young grandson and took over personal responsibility for his education and upbringing. Next, we find Tej studying at the Government College, Mathura, the place of his grandfather's next posting. Tej Bahadur showed his natural brilliance by passing the Matriculation examination at the age of about 15 in 1890 and then shifted to the college in Agra for higher education. There, in 1894, he graduated with first class honours in English, topping the list of the successful candidates. It redounds equally to his credit that in the following year he passed the M.A. examination in English Literature in the first division and also qualified for the degree of the Bachelor of Laws. The story goes that his grandfather tried to get him nominated to the Provincial Civil Service, but this was not to the liking of the young Sapru. The only opening before him was Law and he took it up passionately as his first love and for the rest of his life. He started practice at Moradabad in 1896, a modest beginning indeed for one who was marked out by destiny for the highest legal eminence in later years. Meanwhile, early marriage having been customary those days, Sapru got married in 1890 in a family hailing from Kashmir at a very young age.

Recalling those student days, Sapru noted in later years,[1] "...at the Agra College in the early nineties of the last century, the one political body of which we used to hear a great deal in such newspapers as were then in vogue, was the Congress ... Among the leaders of the Congress of that generation, the four men whose names were most familiar were Surendranath Bannerjee, Lal Mohan Ghose, W.C. Bannerjee and Pandit Ajodhyanath[2] ... My political ideas were of the vaguest and most nebulous character at that time..."

"An event happened in my student days in 1891 which aroused my interest in the Congress. And that was the visit of Pandit Ajodhyanath to Agra ... He spoke in Urdu and that was my first experience of an Urdu orator. His Urdu ... was chaste, refined, full of humour, but distinctly the Urdu of old Delhi. I do not think I can recall any other speech in Urdu of that type or of that eloquence ... unless I make an exception in favour of a speech which I heard in 1897 at Moradabad from Nawab Mohsin-ul-Mulk ... Pandit Ajodhyanath died suddenly in 1892, and later in the year, at the Allahabad Congress, where I sat quietly among the visitors, I saw all the great men of those days ... My interest was thus aroused in the current politics of the country."

That 1892 Allahabad session of the Indian National Congress may have been the first that the young Tej Sapru attended, but it proved to be the first of many, and he soon followed it up to become a Congress delegate in 1896.

It was also during his student days at the Agra College that Sapru came under the influence of Principal Thompson and Professor Andrews[3] and soon became one of the favourite pupils of the latter. "Professor Andrews himself was a great admirer of, and believer in, John Stuart Mill, and he spoke to me several times in terms of the highest praise of Bishen Narayan Dar's writings. It was Professor Andrews of Agra who introduced me to the works of John Stuart Mill and other writers of that school"[4], noted Sapru later. In another context, he recalled that "...when I was a young man of seventeen or eighteen years, the Allahabad University had taken the forward step of prescribing certain books on politics as apart from the course of English, and it was these books which I read with Mr. Andrews. One theory led to the discussion of half a dozen others ... He constantly warned me... 'Take your time. The time will come when you will be able to make up your mind, and when you are able to make up your mind, you will owe it to your judgement to express your opinion freely, whatever may be the consequences'."[5]

When Sapru was in Agra the Indian National Congress had already made its debut in the political field. The organization which came into existence ten years after his birth marked the gradual consolidation of the glimmering political consciousness of a colonial people lying low under an imperialism, then at the peak of its power. It goes greatly to the credit of the Congress that it sought, and successfully too, to canalize that political consciousness into a sense of nationhood, creating unity and oneness in a social set up of medieval discordance and diversity. The British imperial consolidation then at its acme produced the unconscious, and even unintended, effect of paving the way for the birth of the Indian nation. Noticeably, the first Congress President's address made a particular mention of the need of the fuller development of the sentiments of national unity which had originated during Lord Ripon's Viceroyalty. The echoes of this national sentiment then reverberating throughout educated India touched the young impressionable mind of Sapru far too deeply to be dimmed for the rest of his life. Nationalism indeed became his watchword, his forte in all his political efforts and exertions.

It was a modest beginning for the Congress as it took its first timid steps in the political field within a limited frame of reference. More than that, it was certainly not expected of its at that time that the ruling authorities wanted it merely to act as a safety-valve for public discontent. But it was hardly to be expected that political consciousness once roused would just play second fiddle to the rulers or follow the dotted line. It was not long before the Congress became a live wire organization, representing the political ambitions of an awakened Indian people and providing for the first time an all-India forum for the ventilation of their rightful grievances, though with considerable moderation. In such a posture it naturally could not hope to escape bureaucratic displeasure.

Apart from claiming to represent the Indian nation, the Congress put before the people a new faith and a new methodology. Its philosophy was liberalism and its *modus operandi* was constitutional agitation, startlingly novel things indeed in the immediate background of anger, hatred and confrontation. This new political attitude and approach could be clearly traced to the growth of English education and increasing contacts with England and Englishmen. The founding fathers were genuinely impressed by the progressive nature of British liberalism which had backed freedom's cause in many parts of the world. They further discovered that as a champion of popular government, Britain herself had set up a model, namely, the parliamentary system, and was extending its benefits to many of her overseas colonies. The early Congress stalwarts therefore drew their inspiration from British liberalism and opted wholly for the form of government Britain herself had so successfully adopted. As regards the method of pressing their demands, they naturally chose the constitutional path which accorded equally well with their liberal creed and the then prevailing circumstances. Sapru imbibed these ideas at an early age and stuck to them throughout his life in the face of depressing odds and sometimes damping failures.

The Congress was then in the custody of men like W.C. Bannerjee, Dadabhai Naoroji, Dinshaw Wacha, Surendra Nath Bannerjee, Pandit Ayodhyanath and others. In his Recollections and Impressions[6], Sapru speaks of some of these early stalwarts and how they influenced him intellectually and politically. Surendra Nath's oratory was spell binding. He used to speak passionately on Indian unity and Italian unification and was fervently building up the idea of Indian nationalism. No wonder Sapru was deeply impressed by Bannerjee's speeches and was "swept off his feet" by his wonderful eloquence at the Allahabad Congress of 1892 where he also saw W.C. Banerjee, first Indian President of the Congress.[7] Sapru was also influenced by the speeches of Lal Mohan Ghose who incidentally had led a solo deputation to England on behalf of the Indian Association of Calcutta even before the birth of the Congress. Intellectual fall out from these powerful personalities had a profound effect on Sapru's budding mind and brought him out, though still in an academic way, into the exciting world of politics. Sapru's mental horizon began to expand in an atmosphere saturated with the ideas of nationalism and liberalism.

Pandit Ayodhyanath was another impressive figure and an undisputed leader of the Congress in Sapru's home province. At the fourth Congress in Allahabad he was the Chairman of the Reception Committee and made the session a success despite bureaucratic obstructions. Ayodhyanath's Agra visit of 1891 and his fine Urdu speech on that occasion remained an unforgettable memory with Sapru.[8] Pandit Bishen Narayan Dar, who became Congress President in 1911, was another front rank leader to have influenced Sapru much. Sapru himself says that nobody exercised a greater influence on him than Dar who saturated him with the ideas of Mill, Spencer and Huxley.[9]

Among other nationalist leaders, whom Sapru openly acknowledged to having been profoundly influenced by, were M.G. Ranade and G.K. Gokhale. Tej Bahadur Sapru regarded Ranade as one of the greatest intellects and thinkers that India had produced, and admitted to reading avidly everything written by him. "I remember", noted Sapru, "having heard his speech at the Indian Social Conference at Lucknow in 1899, where he kept the audience spell bound by his synthesis of Hindu-Muslim culture.[10] Gokhale was another statesman that the younger Sapru had come to admire, after falling under his spell at the Benares [Banaras] Congress of 1905. The acquaintance deepened into friendship in 1907, when Gokhale visited Allahabad to explain Congress policy. Later that year, after the Surat Congress in December, and split between the 'Moderates' and 'Extremists', Gokhale stayed with Sapru in Allahabad, where Sapru helped him in drafting the Constitution of the Indian National Congress. In subsequent years too, Gokhale stayed at Sapru's home whenever he visited Allahabad. Gokhale, like Ranade, provided a political role model and source of inspiration for Sapru in the years that followed.

In this context it would be relevant to refer to the intimate glimpses he had had of Islamic culture early in his life. His grandfather was very friendly with the great Muslim leader Syed Ahmed Khan with whom he had been at Bijnor as a government servant during the uprising of 1857. In the company of his grandfather, Sapru used to visit him from time-to-time at Aligarh. There he came in close contact with some of the finest representatives of Muslim culture and of the Persian and Urdu literatures, Sapru had a great admiration for Sir Syed as a powerful intellect. He was no less an admirer of Mahmood, Sir Syed's son. "The fact that my grandfather and I were Hindus and they were Muslims, did not matter in the slightest degree so far as social and intellectual contacts were concerned."[11] These contacts helped broaden his sympathies and generated in him his life long secularism and cultural catholicity. Incidentally, he also acquired a rare command over Urdu and Persian.

Sapru belonged to a family which followed the traditional ways of thinking and living. But culturally Sapru grew out of the family tradition to follow his own individual liberal line.

It was in 1896 that the young Tej Bahadur Sapru started his legal practice at Moradabad. Not long afterwards, Pandit Bishen Narayan Dar visited Moradabad to conduct a criminal case and stayed with the young Sapru. "It was one of the most enjoyable fortnights", recalled Sapru, "...[and] while he was still there I made up my mind to shift to Allahabad, as I found that Moradabad was too stagnant for me".[12] The move to Allahabad took place in 1899, where Sapru joined the High Court Bar. He soon made his way in the legal profession here, though over awed and over shadowed and undoubtedly inspired by the sheer talent of the legal luminaries who then practiced at Allahabad.

Allahabad, besides being the administrative capital of the then North Western Provinces and Oudh (soon re-structured to form the United Provinces of Agra and Oudh better known by its abbreviation of U.P.), had already achieved eminence as a city of judges, lawyers, and scholars. "After I joined the [Allahabad] High Court Bar,"[13] wrote Sapru more than forty years later, "I began to realise how unworthy I was then to be a member of the profession which was dominated in those days by men like Conlan ... ; Mr. (afterwards Sir) Charles Alston ... ; Pandit Sunderlal, Munshi Ram Prasad, Mr. Jogendranath Chaudhari and Pandit Motilal Nehru. Sunderlal's knowledge was the despair of us all... Munshi Ram Prasad, a great advocate, remarkable for the brevity of his arguments, was the very embodiment of dignity. Jogendranath Chaudhari was simply brilliant as there have been very few advocates who have spoken in Court that polished literary language which he used to. Pandit Motilal had just come into the front rank. He had an engaging manner, a keen intellect and a great power of constructing theories in his cases ... He and Sunderlal were the two lions in the profession on the civil side... Immediately after them came two young men of those days. One ... was Pandit Madan Mohan Malaviya...The other man was Maulvi Ghulam Mustafa ... Then came Dr. Satish Chandra Bannerjee ...In a sense, he and I were rivals. We were constantly opposed to each other, but there were no two greater friends in private life than he and I...[and] so far as sheer learning in law is concerned the Allahabad Bar has not produced the front and he and I were great friends..."[14]

Others whom Sapru admired for their legal learning and achievements were Sir Walter Colvin, C.C. Dillon, Sir Edward Chamier, Durga Charan Bannerjee, Sir Abdur Raoof, and Nawab Abdul Majid.[15] In later years, Tej Bahadur's eldest son, Prakash Narain [known at home as Raja]; noted that, over the years, his father had known the leading authorities on law, adding: "He was a great admirer of Mr. Justice Mahmood [Syed Ahmed Khan's son], whom he regarded as a genius in the realm of law, Sir Pramoda Charan Bannerji, Sir Bhasham Ayyangar, Sir Asutosh Mookerjee and the Right Honourable Waris Amir Ali".[16]

Much of that lay in the future at the turn of the century, though. In 1901 Sapru went on to take his Honours in Law (later called LL.M.) from Allahabad University, yet again with record marks, and in 1902 he took his doctorate degree (LL.D.) too. As a 'Doctor of Laws', he soon became a part time Lecturer in Law at Muir Central College, affiliated to Allahabad University. Over the next few years Sapru became widely recognised as a good junior, and by 1905 he decided to give up his lecturership as it interfered with his law practice.

It was during these years that Tej Bahadur Sapru became the founder editor of a magazine called the *Allahabad Law Journal*. He was to edit this for several years. He had also become associated with the journal, *The Hindustan Review*, another affiliation that was to be long-lasting. Sapru later recorded how, under Dr. Sachchidananda Sinha's inspiration, "some of us agreed to join him in starting *The Kayastha Samachar*, now called *The Hindustan Review* and later a paper called *The Indian People*. The brunt of the task fell on him; Satish Chandra Bannerjee and I were only co-adjutors."[17]

Besides his legal work, which was already earning him laurels, Sapru took a keen interest in civil rights and politics during the first decade of the 20th century, often playing an active role. Sapru's early years in politics coincided with the partition of Bengal of 1905 and its aftermath, the Aga Khan led Muslim deputation to Viceroy Minto in 1906, and the birth of the All India Muslim League, the 1907 Surat split, and the eventual passing of the Minto Morley Reforms.[18]

Sapru was one of the Honorary Secretaries to the first United Provinces Provincial Conference held in 1907; he supported the resolution demanding repeal of the Bengal Regulation III of 1818 at the Madras Congress of 1908; at the Lahore Congress of 1909 he moved a resolution urging, among other things, the establishment of Executive Councils for the United Provinces; and at the 1910 Allahabad Congress he was critical of the communal representation in the rules under the 1909 Act.[19]

Sapru's fame had already spread by this period. A diary entry made on 18 March, 1908 by Govind Ballabh Pant, then a young student in Allahabad, records satisfaction at having been present at a public gathering where "Sapru delivered a very humorous and at the same time very pithy and patriotic speech"[20] (In contrast, C.F. Andrews has described Sapru's speeches in English as being "terse and closely to the point, without any superfluous words ... [in] the forensic style with which he would plead a case in court. He was a debater rather than an orator, and did not even care to sway the multitudes by emotional appeals"[21]).

By 1910 Sapru enjoyed the reputation of being one of northern India's leading lawyers. He had also begun to win recognition as a political figure. On a personal note, however, the year 1910 was marked by tragedy for him and his children with the death of his wife, Durga. Sapru never remarried. Nor was he ever linked with any other woman in his life, thereafter. In the years that followed, Sapru remained a busy lawyer, who retained a keen interest in national politics.[22] Besides court appearances, his legal opinions were eagerly sought and highly regarded throughout the land. It is scarcely surprisingly, therefore, that when it came to the preparation of what later became the Wakf Bill (Mussalman Wakf Validating Act VI of 1913), which was piloted in the Central Assembly by M.A. Jinnah, and placed on the statute book in 1913, it was Tej Bahadur Sapru, who was invited by his close friend, Maulana Shibli Numani (1857-1914), to draft the Bill.[23]

In March 1913 Tej Bahadur was inducted into the United Provinces Legislative Council, under the Morley Minto Constitution. He was to remain a Member of the Council till 1916. Though a nominated member, Sapru did not invariably toe the official line, as nominated members were usually expected to do at the time. Rather, he put the broad nationalistic point of view, associating himself with progressive proposals, and where necessary, unhesitatingly criticising official measures. "He was thus acting virtually as an independent member with a distinct nationalist leaning."[24] During this period, alongside Council and law related work, Sapru presided over the meetings of the U.P. Social Conference and the U.P. Political Conference in 1913 and 1914. Both were organisations of which he was among the co-founders and long-term secretary.

It was in September 1916 that Sapru was elected on the Congress ticket to India's Imperial Legislative Council, a body of which he was to remain a member until 1922. "Sapru was at his best in the houses of legislature", claims one biographer, "...and easily became one of the stalwarts of the house."[25] Sapru's analytical mind, legal training and keen interest in topical issues enhanced his standing in the Council. According to C.F. Andrews, "No one probably rendered more active help to the Government of India as an adviser at that critical juncture: for Sapru was as blunt of speech as he was independent of character."[26]

In October 1916, a representation was presented to the Viceroy by nineteen non-official members of the Imperial Legislative Council. Now referred to as the 'Memorandum of 19', it called for 'Representative Government' and 'Dominion Status' for India, and embodied the national demand for constitutional reforms. Tej Bahadur Sapru was not merely one of its signatories; apparently the memorandum was principally drafted and formulated by him along with Jinnah and Malaviya.[27]

Sapru was also among the vocal supporters of the resolution of self-government at the Lucknow Congress held in December 1916, and played a prominent part along with Jinnah, Wazir Hasan and others, to bring about a Pact between the Congress and the Muslim League regarding the future constitution for India. This agreement at Lucknow became embodied in the Congress League Lucknow Pact. The parties jointly demanded a legislative assembly for India to be elected on a communal basis. Furthermore, the Pact accepted the principle of separate electorates for the Muslim community, and it was agreed that in five out of the seven provinces Muslims would be given over-representation.

He was one of the pillars of Mrs. Annie Besant's Home Rule League. His agitations, when Mrs. Besant was incarcerated in June 1917, which went to the extent of his threatening to court arrest, were largely responsible for her ultimate release.[28] He was one of the Indian leaders interviewed by Secretary of State Edwin Montagu during his visit to India in 1917, in regard to constitutional reforms. After the publication of the Montagu Chelmsford Report in April 1918, differences between the so-called moderates and extremists came to the fore. Seceding from the National Congress in 1918, Sapru was one of the founding members of the moderate party, later called the National Liberal Federation of India. In March 1919 he was elected President of U.P. Liberal Association and was appointed one of the General Secretaries of the Party. He was a member of Lord South-borough's Functions Committee (1918), appointed for the purposes of the reforms, and in 1919 he appeared as a witness before Lord Selborne's Committee in London. While still a member of the Legislative Council, he was appointed Law Member of the Governor General's Executive Council and assumed office on December 22, 1920. Early in 1923 he resigned as a protest against Mahatma Gandhi's imprisonment and to dedicate himself thereafter to India's constitutional advancement. Later in the year he represented India at the Imperial (now the Commonwealth) Conference and successfully crossed swords with General Smuts, the South African Prime Minister, on citizenship rights of Indians settled abroad. In December 1923 he presided over the session of the National Liberal Federation at Poona. As a non-official member of the Reforms Enquiry Committee of 1924 he drafted[29] famous minority report with Jinnah as one of its signatories and demanded from Government that the constitution must be placed on a permanent basis with an in-built mechanism for automatic advance towards Dominion Status. On the eve of the minority report he also wrote his book *The Indian Constitution* (Adyar, Madras, published in 1926). As President of the National Convention with Mrs. Besant as the General Secretary, he drafted the Swaraj scheme which was completed in December 1924. The scheme under the title "A Bill to Constitute within the British Empire a Commonwealth of India" was presented to the House of Commons by George Lansbury in 1925. Jinnah was a signatory and supporter of the scheme.

In 1927 he presided over the Bombay session of the National Liberal Federation of India. In his address he was the first Indian leader to call for a national boycott of the all white Simon Commission. He appealed for a closing of ranks to forge Indian unity and to produce an agreed constitution to meet Birkenhead's challenge that Indians were incapable of framing a constitution for themselves. Thus the All Parties Conference of 1928 appointed a committee, with Motilal Nehru as chairman to prepare a constitution. Sapru was its most expert member and though the Report of the Committee was named after its chairman, Sapru was the main author.[30] In the Sapru-Nehru Report (as it should be termed), he visualized a federal polity for the whole of India inclusive of the princely states. After producing the Report he created the opportunity[31] for calling a round table conference between Indian interests and British political parties. This was the result of his discussions with Viceroy Irwin in March 1929 and he was persuaded to follow the line by the old guard of the Congress, particularly, Motilal Nehru himself.[32] At the pressure of Jawaharlal Nehru and the radicals, Congress repudiated its earlier stand in support of the Irwin announcement, demanded complete independence, and decided to launch the civil disobedience movement on a massive scale. "In perspective", Nehru's biographer points out, "the controversy over Dominion status and complete independence was over a straw man for there is no substantive difference between them."[33] Every effort was made by Sapru to persuade Congress to participate in the conference. After mediation failed, Sapru with Jinnah's support led the movement to consolidate the forces that stood for Dominion Status. In the teeth of vehement opposition from Congress they went to London and attended the First Round Table Conference in 1930. There Sapru forged Indian unity, enlisted the support of the leading princes, projected the ideal of an All India Federation and demanded responsible government at the Centre. Every Indian interest, except the Congress which was absent, supported his demand. His victory was complete when Lord Reading, British Liberal Party delegate to the Conference, converted by Sapru's influence, lent his support that turned the balance in favour of constitutional advance for India. "No man has done so much as you", wrote Sir Francis Younghusband to Sapru, "to turn British public opinion in favour of India".[34] In doing so Sapru defeated the diehard attack against Indian freedom. Federation was the Trojan horse that helped make a breach in the citadel of power.

While still in London he resigned from the Liberal Federation and till the end of his days functioned as an independent statesman. Armed with Prime Minister MacDonald's declaration that "With a Legislature constituted on a Federal basis, His Majesty's Government will be prepared to recognize the principle of the responsibility of the Executive to the Legislature", he returned to India and was the decisive factor in bringing about the Gandhi-Irwin Pact. Mahatma Gandhi's participation in the Second Round Table Conference in 1931 is a measure of his success. By participating in the Third Round Table Conference in 1932 and the Joint Parliamentary Committee in 1933 he laboured to protect the emerging constitution from diehard onslaught against liberalization of safeguards and in doing so made it less reactionary than what it otherwise would have been. His great contribution to all the Round Table Conferences that resulted in the Act of 1935 is highlighted by Lord Chancellor Sankey as follows: "I greatly value what you say about my work at the Indian Round Table Conference, but, if you will allow me to say so, it was nothing compared with your own ... I have always felt it was you who assembled the material, or, in other words it was you who supplied the ideas, the knowledge, and experience which others made use of. Personally I regret that Constitution did not go as for as it would have gone if all your ideas had been accepted, but, nonetheless, they remain for future guidance and use."[35]

As President of the U.P. Unemployment Committee he wrote comprehensive report which revealed how anxious he was to launch India in the wake of the Act of 1935 on the constructive road to economic prosperity. He laboured boldly in spite of overwhelming opposition from political parties for the early establishment of a federal government at the Centre. It was his thesis that despite all its shortcomings the Act of 1935 must be worked and whatever power had devolved must be grasped both at the Centre and the provinces simultaneously. He was emphatic in his warning of not accepting provincial autonomy without accepting responsibility at the Centre also, for therein lay the seeds of disruption.

Jinnah, fearing perpetual Hindu domination at the Centre was the first to reject the federal part of the new constitution. Taking advantage of the supposed suppression of minority rights by the 1937 Congress ministries, he gathered mass Muslim support and added a formidable dimension to the communal problem. In 1939 when the world war started, Linlithgow suspended the establishment of Federation. As Sapru saw, it was a 'fateful decision' that unleashed fissiparous forces. In the stormy period that followed he formed the Non-Party Conference with a view to surmount the communal rift and to force the Churchill Government to move forward. His cable to Churchill in January 1942 inaugurated a fresh phase of negotiations with the British, starting with the Cripps Mission and culminating in the final transfer of power. During this period Gandhi turned to Sapru more and more to resolve the communal threat thrust by intransigence of Jinnah. After the 1942 Gandhian movement which Sapru tried to prevent, for therein he feared the strengthening of separatist forces while Congress leaders were in prison, Sapru kept alive the spirit of the nation by fighting in his own inimitable way British immobility. Later, after the failure of the Gandhi-Jinnah talks, with Gandhi's tacit approval and support he formed his Conciliation Committee, raised the issue of Pakistan to a scientific level, wrote his monumental report of 1945, rejected the claim for India's disruption and laid down guidelines for the permanent democratic constitution of India. Soon he became seriously ill and after his interview with the Cabinet Mission he became bed ridden. He had to decline his seat offered by Jawaharlal Nehru on the Constituent Assembly but he was always available for informal discussions. Events moved swiftly and Pakistan became a reality. He had an acute sense of helplessness in a crisis that called for the exercise of all his powers. In June 1947 a close friend wrote to him: "Just as you having lived the cleanest and most virtuous of lives, did not deserve your present affliction, so also innocent unoffending India does not deserve its impending chaos."[36]

And Sapru wrote back: "I am afraid the division of India is not going to be the end of our trouble. I fear that may be it is the beginning of a new trouble which may last for a quarter of a century. It is not easy to say what Congress or the Hindus should have done to enforce their demand for the preservation of the political unity of India."[37]

Sapru's personality represented a rich synthesis. He was a rebel of a sort against the traditionalism of his family and of the times. He had a fine schooling in English literature and imbibed a good deal from the Western culture. But he was not completely cut-off from the Indian traditional culture. Indeed his was an open mind absorbing and assimilating whatever he thought was of value radiating from the Eastern as well as the Western culture. Similarly his contact with the Islamic civilization contributed significantly to his catholicity and socially liberal frame of mind. Politically he drank deep at the fountain of European liberalism. But socially he was a radical opposed to the barriers of caste and creed and other kinds of inhibitions. It is interesting to note that the Indian political and social reform movements went for a long time *pari passu*—for many years the annual Congress sessions and those of the Indian Social Conference synchronized. Also, our political liberals were by and large socially progressive, while the political radicals were often tied to the past. Sapru was also like that, a moderate politician with advanced social views.

REFERENCES

1. Raina, K.N. and V. Gopala Ratnam (eds.), *Tej Bahadur Sapru: Profiles and Tributes* (Allahabad: The Indian Press Pvt. Ltd.), 1971, pp. 263-264.
2. Pandit Ajodhyanath's son, Hirday Nath Kunzru, was among Sapru's close associates.
3. Professor Andrews, a Cambridge Educated Indian Christian, is different from the Rev. C.F. (Charlie) Andrews.
4. Raina, K.N. and V. Gopala Ratnam (eds.), *Tej Bahadur Sapru: Profiles and Tributes, op. cit.*
5. Sapru's Speech at Agra College on 25 Feburary 1934, reprinted in *Agra College Magazine*, Vol. IX, No. 3, April 1934.
6. Raina, K.N. and V. Gopala Ratnam (eds.), *Tej Bahadur Sapru: Profiles and Tributes, op. cit.*
7. Broadcast Talk, All India Radio, Lucknow, December 8, 1941, published under 'T.C. Miscellany' in Twentieth Century, January 1942.
8. Raina, K.N. and V. Gopala Ratnam (eds.), *Tej Bahadur Sapru: Profiles and Tributes, op. cit.*
9. Broadcast Talk, All India Radio, Lucknow, December 8, 1941, published under 'T.C. Miscellany' in Twentieth Century, January 1942.
10. Raina, K.N. and V. Gopala Ratnam (eds.), *Tej Bahadur Sapru: Profiles and Tributes, op. cit.*, p. 266.
11. Broadcast Talk, All India Radio, Lucknow, December 8, 1941, published under 'T.C. Miscellany' in Twentieth Century, January 1942.
12. Raina, K.N. and V. Gopala Ratnam (eds.), *Tej Bahadur Sapru: Profiles and Tributes, op. cit.*
13. *Ibid.*, pp. 268-269.
14. *Ibid.*
15. Sapru's Presidential Address, *First United Provinces of Agra and Oudh Lawyers' Conference,* Allahabad, 6-7, November 1938, p. 14.
16. Raina (ed.), *Tej Bahadur Sapru—Responsa: Selected Legal Opinions* (Bombay: N.M. Tripathi Pvt. Ltd.), 1976, p. xiii.
17. Raina, K.N. and V. Gopala Ratnam (eds.), *Tej Bahadur Sapru: Profiles and Tributes, op. cit.*, p. 269.
18. Chandra, Bipin *et al.*, *India's Struggle for Independence, 1857-1947* (New Delhi: Penguin Books), 1989.
19. Bose, *Tej Bahadur Sapru* (New Delhi: Publications Division, Government of India), 1978, pp. 16-24.
20. Nanda, B.R. (ed.), *Selected Works of Gobind Ballabh Pant*, Vol. I (New Delhi: Oxford University Press), 1993, p. 89.
21. Williams, Rushbrook (ed.), *Great Men of India*, Home Library Club, 1940, p. 396.
22. Bose, *Tej Bahadur Sapru, op. cit.*, pp. 8-32.
23. Raina, K.N. and V. Gopala Ratnam (eds.), *Tej Bahadur Sapru: Profiles and Tributes, op. cit.*, p. 267.

24. Bose, *Tej Bahadur Sapru, op. cit.*, p. 28.
25. *Ibid.*, p. 37.
26. Williams, Rushbrook (ed.), *Great Men of India, op. cit.*, p. 397.
27. Raina (ed.), *Welding the Nation* (Bombay: N.M. Tripathi Pvt. Ltd.), 1976, p. xv.
28. Manuscript of a short biography of Dr. Tej Bahadur Sapru by late Justice P.N. Sapru (unpublished).
29. Sir R.P. Paranjpye to Justice P. N. Sapru (from a letter of condolence), Poona, January 21, 1949.
30. Wilson, F.W., *The Indian Chaos* (London: London Press), 1932.
31. Manuscript of a short biography of Dr. Tej Bahadur Sapru by late Justice P.N. Sapru (unpublished).
32. Sapru-Jayakar Correspondence, Sapru Papers deposited to the Government of India, National Library (Calcutta: Belvedere), 2 series.
33. Michael, Brecher, *Nehru—A Political Biography* (London: London Press), 1959, p. 134.
34. Sir Francis Younghusband to Sapru, London, July 27, 1932.
35. Lord Sankey to Sapru, London, February 24, 1937, Sapru Papers deposited to the Government of India, National Library, *op. cit.*
36. Sir K.N. Haskar to Sapru, Sapru Papers deposited to the Government of India, National Library, *op. cit.*
37. Sapru to K.N. Haskar, Sapru Papers deposited to the Government of India, National Library, June, 1947, *op. cit.*

2

POLITICAL ORIENTATION

During the first decade of the 20th century many events of a far-reaching significance for Indian politics took place. By 1905 the Indian National Congress was 20 years old with an impressive record of activity to its credit. It had helped rouse political consciousness in the name of Indian nationhood, and in a country of almost baffling diversity, forged the idea of an Indian unity. With their firm faith in the British sense of justice and fairness, the founding fathers of the Congress had urged various administrative reforms and pleaded for an increasing share for Indians in it. Not only that. They had made their voice reach the policy making Chambers of Whitehall. It is easy to belittle the Moderates' achievements. But the panorama of events from 1885 to 1905 shows a great revolution in the thoughts and ideas of the people they had been instrumental in paving the way for the more radical movements of the later days. The Moderate leaders thus did have an impressive record of achievement. It stands greatly to their credit that they built up India's organized public life and made it distinct with a new urge and aspiration. They were indeed the active agents for ushering in the striking change in public mind that marked the transition from the past century to the present. "They, it is that have made possible the super-structure, storey by storey, of colonial self-government, Home Rule within the Empire, Swaraj and, on top of all, complete independence".[1]

But the public mood was rapidly changing and the placid politics of the Moderates was failing to measure up to the raising political demands and expectations. Owing to a number of factors, a school of opinion arose towards the end of the last century, mainly under the leadership of Tilak, which would no longer be satisfied with the "mendicancy" of the Congress. Tilak had come out with a powerful challenge during his lifetime. With the dawning of the 20th century, the trend gathered a rapid momentum, and by 1905 streams of neo-nationalism flowing from Maharashtra and Bengal converged into one great wave of seething unrest.

Gokhale, the central figure of the Moderate milieu, had left an abiding impression upon the mind and thoughts of Sapru. They were kindred spirits, both having drunk deep from the same fountainhead, that is, Ranade. With all his idealism Gokhale was a practical realist. So was Sapru. Gokhale knew very well that at that stage of political evolution the British would not part with any substantial measure of power, as was evident from the niggardly Reforms of 1909, about which Gokhale himself had negotiated with Morley. He was therefore satisfied, for the moment, with trying to harmonize the desperate elements of public life so as to be able to bargain for progressive Indian participation in the administration. Without going after what was theoretically desirable, he was content, for the time being of course, with what was practically feasible and thus advised the acceptance of the Morley-Minto Reforms, pleading simultaneously for gradualness and agitation through constitutional channels. It is interesting to think how faithfully Sapru assimilated this political approach and style of working.

Sapru's entry into politics was unostentatious. He became spontaneously politics-oriented early in his life when he heard or came in touch with, some of the giants of those days. By 1906 he had established himself as one of the most promising juniors at the Bar and could find time to make some amateurish sallies into politics, until he started making more mature responses to his second love. At the Benaras Congress of 1905, he came under the spell of Gokhale, the year's President, a spell that never really left him. Sapru refers to him as a man "under whose spell I had come about that time and whom I still hold as the most constructive statesman of our times".[2] Reminiscing in a different context Sapru says: "Mr. Gokhale came to Allahabad in 1907 to explain the Congress policy. He had undertaken a tour for this purpose and he inaugurated a series of speeches at Allahabad. On the day he made his first speech, he did not allow any visitor to call on him between 10 a.m. and 4 p.m. as he had to prepare his speech. Three or four years later, he came to Allahabad once again and I found him similarly absorbed in his work. The occasion was the preparation of a paper for the Universal Races Congress. Read that even today. Every word in it is precious; if young men follow Gokhale's ways they will assuredly be benefited. Barring one or two men I cannot think of a person so well-informed and well-posted in the theoretical as well as practical aspects of Indian politics as Ghokale".[3] Sapru thus came very close to the elder statesman who, while at Allahabad, used to be Sapru's guest. Gokhale and Sapru were the representative of what may be called the Ranade School of thought.

Like Gokhale, Sapru was by character and temperament averse to extra-constitutional means and believed that the constitutional method of agitation was the best under the circumstances, even though that might mean a painful gradualness in the attainment of our national objective. Speaking at Allahabad on February 4, 1907, Gokhale had said that "redress must be obtained through the constituted authority" and that "the idea that we should leave the authorities severally alone and seek to attain our goal independently of them is inadmissible and absurd".[4] Both Gokhale and Sapru were wholly averse to violence, lawlessness and seditious methods and both believed in the destiny of India as a part of the British Commonwealth.

The formative years of Sapru's political life were also the days of the organized beginnings of Muslim separatism. The Aga Khan delegation of 1906 earned from a willing Minto and an unwilling Morley separate representation for the Muslims. This was followed by the birth of the Muslim League which spearheaded the separatist demand till the partition of the country. As a token of his firm faith in secularism and communal conciliation, Gokhale even initially welcomed the formation of the Muslim League hoping that it would work in a constructive spirit. He was prepared to concede special supplementary representation to the Muslims over and above the general representation, while not being in favour of separate electorates. So was Sapru a life long crusader for communal harmony and conciliation. Gokhale died in 1915. But Sapru was destined to carry on his mission.

A flashback to the political conditions then obtaining in Sapru's home province would not be irrelevant here. Despite the fact that public life in the United Provinces of Agra and Oudh was slow to catch up with the new spirit compared to the Presidencies, signs of animation were unmistakably in evidence even towards the end of the last century. To the second Congress at Calcutta in 1886, U.P. sent 74 delegates, the largest contingent next to Bengal "marking the enlightenment of the great Province which contains Lucknow, Cawnpur, Agra, Allahabad, Benaras, Bareilly, Meerut—great centres of thought".[5] Allahabad hosted the fourth Congress where the presence of U.P.'s 583 delegates signified an awakened public life. And the session was made possible in the face of stiff official opposition. In less than five years' time, to be specific in 1892, Allahabad played the host to another session of the national organization. And then again the fifteenth Congress took place in Lucknow in 1899—about the time when Sapru had just joined the High Court Bar.

That U.P.'s political horizon was fast expanding was evident from the number of conferences held in the Province from the beginning of the last century. "The conferences held at Allahabad were the first of their kind. It was a matter of just reproach against these Provinces that they considerably lagged behind other provinces in public spiritedness, that they had no associations and held no conferences. It must be a source of satisfaction to all, that at last the reproach has been removed".[6] Motilal Nehru presided over the first U.P. Provincial Conference in 1907 and Sapru was one of the Honorary Secretaries. The second conference held in 1908 in the context of the Surat split was presided over by Madan Mohan Malaviya. Bishen Narayan Dar was another shining light of the conference. Through all these thrilling experiences Sapru was having the first taste of public life and also maturing politically.

Among the U.P. leaders Ayodhyanath was the most eminent. He was the Chairman of the Reception Committee of the fourth Congress. Then there were other luminaries like Bishambhar Nath, Bishen Narayan Dar, and Ganga Prasad of Lucknow on the political scene. Malaviya was of course a towering personality. "It was he who in conjunction with Babu Ganga Prasad Verma kept the Congress flag flying in the United Provinces in all those years".[7] The eminence of Motilal Nehru as a Congress leader is well known. He became President of the first U.P. Provincial Conference when he was 46. He started taking more seriously to politics from 1917 onwards when he was fairly advanced in age. Initially a man of moderate views, he, like Sapru, joined the Home Rule Movement started by Dr. Annie Besant. U.P. politics was till then firmly in the control of the Moderates.

Nevertheless tension was building up. The partition of Bengal and the events coming in its wake, had inevitably their impact on Upper India rousing people to a new consciousness of national dignity and solidarity. The *Indian People* of Allahabad (October 5, 1905) spoke of the power of the *Swadeshi* movement to unify the different "peoples" of the country into a homogenous whole.

It is well known that the Bengal partition gave an impetus to the growth of extremism in the country, and U.P. was not left entirely unaffected. By 1907 when the anti-partition movement was at its peak and a Moderate Extremist split was looming large on the horizon, the new spirit of radicalism spread to U.P. as well. In 1907 several all-India leaders of both the Moderate and the Extremist schools visited Allahabad and a few other U.P. cities, and they were Gokhale, Lajpat Rai, Bipin Chandra Pal and Tilak. People were swept away by their eloquence. Tilak's speech on "Our Present Situation" in which he said, "*Swadeshi* is the first step, boycott is the means and *Swaraj* is the end", created a great impact, specially on the youth who seemed, by and large, to be inclined towards the Extremist camp. The citizens of Allahabad (November 11, 1907) spoke of the political triumvirate of Tilak, Gokhale and Pal having been invited to Allahabad as if to counteract one school of politics with another. The *Indian People* (March 24, 1907) spoke of the division of the Allahabad citizens into Moderate and Extremist and blamed Tilak for this. Allahabad, Sapru's home town, was the epicentre of U.P.'s political awakening. However, despite Extremist pressure, U.P. politics continued to be in the custody of the Moderates including Sapru. After the Surat split which found Sapru irrevocably on the side of the Moderates, his home at Allahabad became the haunt of the elder leaders.

Sapru started taking interest in Congress politics quite early in his career. At the Lahore Congress of 1900 he was made a member of its Education Committee along with Malaviya, Dar and others. At the Madras, Congress of 1908 held immediately after the Surat split, Sapru lent a powerful support to a resolution demanding the repeal of the Bengal Regulation III of 1818. Criticising the Regulation in strong terms he said that it was against the very first principle of English jurisprudence. He said: "I would go further and say that it constitutes a very great menace to our liberty. It stands hanging over our heads like the sword of Damocles".[8] In the 1909 Lahore Congress, he moved a resolution urging the establishment of Executive Councils for the United Provinces, among others a point he had occasion to revert to again and again.

The first decade of the current century was a period of great unrest to which not a small contribution was made by Curzon, among other things, by his bureaucratic politico-surgery on Bengal. The forces of neo-nationalism grouped themselves under the inspiring leadership of the Lal-Bal-Pal triumvirate with Aurbindo Ghosh providing the theatrical scaffolding. Acts of terrorism became widespread and not necessarily in Bengal. These brought in their wake the most drastic retaliation from the Government. Men of the eminence of Lajpat Rai were deported under Regulation III. In fact the Moderates found the situation extremely embarrassing for themselves and were often on the defensive. The surging tide of neo-nationalism which made its inroad into the Benaras Congress of 1905 threatened to engulf the organization's Calcutta session of 1906. Finally came the Surat split throwing the Moderates into the dilemma of pursuing their own constitutional course, while still remaining active in the mainstream of the national life. This was difficult to do in the circumstances then prevailing. However from 1908 to 1914, Tilak was in Mandalay jail leaving the Moderates a comparatively easy field to function in. Then the war years intervened followed by a relative lull which however was really on the surface and was broken soon enough. Political militancy raised its head again inviting the most drastic measures from the Government to suppress any manifestation of it. The final parting of ways between the Moderates and the Extremists came inevitably in 1917.

The Government's paltry gesture of conciliation which was also meant to keep the Moderates in good humour came first in the shape of the Indian Councils Act of 1909 and then in that of the annulment of the partition of Bengal. Side by side, Minto sowed the seeds of communal disharmony which were so dangerously to affect the destiny of the country.

The 1908 session of the Congress welcomed the Reforms proposals hoping that they would be worked in a liberal spirit. But in 1910 the Congress was keenly disappointed to see the ugly face of communalism peeping out of the detailed regulations meant to work the Reforms. Even Gokhale who had with his robust optimism called the Reforms, a great step forward, could not help noticing that the Regulations had caused very great dissatisfaction throughout the country except in the Mohamedan circles.

At the twenty fifth Congress held in Allahabad (1910) at Sapru's request, some aspects of the communal representation in the Reforms scheme were strongly criticised. Sapru himself was highly critical of the unjust communal weightage given under the scheme. He said: "I have never thought that separate electorates are a blessing. On the contrary I have always maintained and I do still maintain that it would be to the best interest of the country if we could so arrange our affairs that joint electorates were to become possible and even probable ... What we maintain is that we the Hindus, Mohamedans, Christians and Parsis are all equal subjects of the King. Being equal subjects of the King we claim it as our birth-right that each one of us for political purposes be considered equal ... We say by all means let the Mohamedan community and let every other community have as much say as is their due but not at the expense of any other community".[9] These observations, reflect Sapru's and his fellow Moderates' unmistakable frustration at the way the Regulations framed under the 1909 Act gave undue weightage to the representation of the Muslims, described in a Congress resolution as an anomalous distinction between different classes of His Majesty's subjects.

At the Lucknow Congress of 1916, Sapru supporting a resolution on self-government said: "Reforms in driblets and instalments we have had in the past and we might expect to have in future. They will not satisfy the growing aspirations of our countrymen now. Self-respect alone demands that like other self-respecting nations of the world we should be allowed to have a free hand to work out our own destiny and that we should not be treated as perpetual school boys in politics.....Time for that has gone by".[10]

Acknowledging that Tej Bahadur firmly believed in the so-called 'Moderate school of Indian political thought', his eldest son, P.N. Sapru, stressed that the term 'Moderate', *does them* less than justice. "They were definitely not moderate in their aspirations for their country", he averred. "They wanted it to rise to the full height of its stature ... They had a sense of pride in their glorious history and while they had no prejudices against the West and were prepared to assimilate the best that the West had to offer ... they wanted their country to preserve what was best in her heritage and not be an imitation of Europe. The liberal school to which my father belonged represented the old Congress, the Congress of Dadabhai Naoroji, Gokhale and Surendra Nath Bannerjee as modified after 1916 by contact with Annie Besant and Tilak ... it was not until 1919 that he parted company with the Congress, but even after he had severed his connection with it, his relations with Congress leaders, and more especially with Gandhiji were of a most cordial nature"[11]

Elsewhere P.N. Sapru noted that: "Perhaps the Liberals of that generation were dominated by the idea that India's destiny was linked with that of Britain ... But any student of Constitutional history knows that dominion status as visualised by them was in no way different from complete Independence or in Mahatma Gandhi's phrase 'the substance of Independence'. As a jurist and scholar of Constitutional Law, father had hardly any equal in the country, and in accepting dominion status as the aim for which they must work he was not in any way different from Tilak or Bipin Chandra Pal or Lajpat Rai or C.R. Das (with whom he carried weight) or Motilal Nehru who was a cautious man in politics and was a staunch supporter of the Gokhale school of thought. It must not be understood that he wanted for his country a status lower than that of any independent country ... His moderation, if it can be described as moderation, was studied. The only difference between him and the Congress leaders was that he held that if we gave the British the impression of being irrevocably anti-British even though they may depart this country, they may leave us in a position which would weaken us permanently. Nevertheless he was an unsparing critic of the British Government which had always respected him."[12]

Sapru had by that time fairly established himself in law and was politically growing up. His rich and varied personality was unfolding itself in different directions. At about this time he suffered a severe personal loss. That was in 1910. Sapru was away in Bijnor to look after his ailing youngest son when his beloved wife who was in the family way fell critically ill. Within barely a few hours of his return to Allahabad, she expired plunging the whole family into profound grief. Sapru was deeply devoted to his wife who, in her turn, exercised considerable influence on him. It was a stunning tragedy for Sapru who was then only 35 years of age. Motilal Nehru is said to have taken him to Mussoorie for change and diversion. But the grief was inconsolable.

Soon after, Sapru realized that work was the only cure for sorrow. Accordingly he sought to get over the pangs of bereavement by plunging himself into work both professional and public. Although he lost his wife so early in life, he never married again, nor felt interested in the company of women. He was in this respect shy and retiring, and indeed a puritan at heart. It was work, incessant work, with which he filled the vacuum of his life.

In this context Sapru's keen interest in the newspaper press which he developed early in his life, is worth mentioning. Wedded completely to democracy and the parliamentary system of government, he looked upon the press as the greatest bulwark of the same. In this respect he was faithfully following in the footsteps of his elders in the Congress who, having an equally ardent faith in the role of the newspaper press, sought close associations with it or either owned or edited it for projecting their own political opinions.

Early in his life he is known to have been a writer for the *Kayastha Samachar*, an educational magazine edited under the auspices of the *Kayastha Pathshala,* first by Ramananda Chatterji and later by Dr. Sachchidananda Sinha, Sapru's life long friend. When in 1900 the magazine was rechristened the *Hindustan Review* under Sinha's stewardship, Sapru collaborated with him in running it. In this connection Sinha himself says: "With this issue the *Hindustan Review* enters upon the fiftieth year of its existence. Its first issue appeared in 1900 from Allahabad. The place of honour in it was given to a young publicist lawyer who attempted a survey of the administration of the then Lieutenant-Governor of the North-Western Provinces and Oudh... That young publicist and quite a junior lawyer at that time was Pandit Tej Bahadur Sapru, afterwards the Right Hon'ble Sir Tej Bahadur Sapru..."[13]

Sapru was also associated with the conversion of Sinha's tri-weekly *Indian People* into the daily *Leader*. Sapru was one of its Founder Directors and later the Chairman of its Board of Directors. What is more interesting to note, he did quite a bit of freelancing by writing frequently for the *Leader*.

This way he developed a good deal of friendship with C.Y. Chintamani, distinguished editor of the *Leader* and a top ranking Liberal politician of those days. The friendship stood the strain of some major political differences which centred round what was supposed to be Sapru's too much accommodation to the Muslim point of view and to the Princes in the proposed federal scheme. All these appear to have led to Sapru's resignation from the Liberal party in the early thirties, but the friendship continued. Chintamani pays Sapru a fine tribute, saying: "He is a true friend and has a generous heart and many endearing personal qualities."[14]

Sapru never lost his early interest in the press. Decades later he was the guiding spirit behind the publication of the *Twentieth Century* magazine in 1934 under the editorship of K. Iswara Dutt. He and Dutt planned it on a national perspective and made it a vehicle of independent thinking. Sapru was a frequent contributor to it, often under his own signature and sometimes under pen-name. Dutt himself says: "Sapru's word acquired a significance of its own in those days when independence of judgment compelled greater attention than inspired party eloquence".[15] Sapru was indeed a publicist in his own right and not by courtesy. Apart from that, he was ever zealous of the liberty of the press which he thought was an integral part of a society's democratic structure. This would be evident, among other things, from his stout defence of editors in several newspaper contempt cases.

Side by side he was gaining ascendency in local affairs and local politics. He became associated with the Allahabad University as a member of its Senate and Syndicate. He presided over the U.P. social and political conferences in 1913 and 1914 respectively. In 1913 he was nominated a member of the U.P. Legislative Council, a forum where he had the first opportunity to show his parliamentary skill. As a nominated member of the Council he had his many embarrassing moments, because with his natural independence of spirit, he could not toe the official line in all cases, as the nominated members those days were expected to do. On the other hand, he put forward the broad nationalistic point of view and heartily associated himself with all progressive proposals. Where necessary he did not hesitate to criticise the official measures. He was thus acting virtually as an independent member with a distinct nationalist leaning. The functions of the non-official members were severely limited under the then Constitution. Indeed the so-called non-official majority granted by the same was illusory, because it was composed of both the elected and the nominated members, and the nominated members usually sided with the Government. Under the then prevailing system, the non-official members used to be reduced to a minority against the official and the nominated members combined. But on many occasions Sapru sided with the elected members in putting forward proposals which went against the Government point of view. Needless to say that such proposals were often frustrated by the built in majority the Government commanded in the House. But the indefatigable champion of the public cause was definitely emerging in the Council House of U.P.

Sapru was fully aware of the innate insufficiency of the constitutional provisions in this regard and pleaded for a real non-official majority. He said: "... Unless the constitution of this Council is more liberalized and unless we realize that we have power not only to speak but also to give effect to our decisions, I do not think that there is much reason for congratulation"[16] Indeed he would have been happy to have an elected majority. When a resolution to this effect was moved in the Council, Sapru, though embarrassed as a nominated member, supported it, saying: "My sympathies are with the mover of the resolution."[17]

The non-official members' important demands, for example, for an Executive Council for U.P., could not get acceptance because of the unreal nature of the non-official majority. On the floor of the Council Sapru pleaded strongly for such an Executive Council but without any result. He was sadly disappointed at the rejection of such proposals because of the non-official elements failing to muster adequate strength.

As a legislator Sapru found education, notably Primary Education, sadly neglected in his home province and never allowed any let up in his effort to promote its cause. The Government then was a law and order one, a police raj, so to say, which had no pretension about doing anything in particular for the socio-economic uplift of the people. Because of the educational lag in his home province and also because of the official indifference to it, Sapru tried vigorously to slash budget expenditures on less important items, and particularly on police, and divert the same to Education. Immediately on his induction into the Council in March 1913, he moved a resolution demanding that "the allotment for Education for 1913-14 be raised by Rs. 1,00,000 for the opening of 600 additional primary schools and that the allotment to Police be reduced by that amount."[18] He demanded more and better schools and encouraged private enterprise in promoting education. He emphasised that it was useless to put Indian Educational Service men as headmasters in schools unless the quality of education at the bottom, that is, in the lower forms, was improved. Fully aware of the poor state of female education in U.P., he repeatedly stressed that it must be encouraged, despite its prevailing unpopularity. Sapru's untiring stress on the expansion of female education even at the risk of being unpopular brings out his bold and forward looking spirit.

A revenue increase on account of excise duty under 'Country Liquor' in the 1913-14 budget drew from Sapru a caustic comment: "An ordinary layman will certainly read in it an increased moral depravity. The argument that the more you drink, the more prosperous you are may be quite true, but in my opinion the more you drink, the more degraded you are."[19] Regretting the enormous dimension of the drink evil among the lower classes of people, he reminded the official agencies of their duty in the matter. "I think, Sir, in a matter like this the Government should place itself at the head of this social reform movement. That will be the test by which the intention of the Government will be judged by an ordinary man." Like Gandhiji he was against the drink evil. A believer in social reform, he like other Liberals did not think the official agency unwanted in that sphere.

An interesting episode throwing light on Sapru's socio-economic outlook may be recalled here. When Raja Kushal Pal Singh moved a resolution in the Council demanding four seats for the representatives of the landed aristocracy who, he claimed, were the natural leaders of the people, Sapru strongly repudiated the claim. He retorted that throughout the Indian history, it is the man of character, the man of sacrifice, who had been looked upon by the people as their leaders. With the possible exception of Buddha, he said, there was not any other instance of any great landed aristocrat joining the vanguard of progress in the country. "I say those people alone are entitled to be the natural leaders who work for the people and who are in sympathy with the tenants who dwell in the cottages. It is not the zamindars who dwell in the cottages: they dwell in palaces and forts." Sapru was a close friend of many members of the landed aristocracy and many rulers of the Princely States. Quite a number of them were his clients. Many others held him in high esteem. But Sapru had no sympathy with the outdated feudal order. A thoroughly modern man, he wanted the landed aristocracy to attune itself to the modern spirit.

On political questions the future Sapru was in the making. A point made by a Council member regarding Hindu-Muslim representation drew from Sapru the following remark: "For my part I have held this view for many years that if the Mohamedan community thinks that its political salvation lies in separate representation, it is the duty of every Hindu not to offer any opposition to the demand for separate representation. ... but while I am prepared to concede that if the Mohamedan community wants separate representation we should not oppose it, I am not prepared to concede the claim for any excessive representation." This was an obvious reference to the disproportionate weightage given to the Muslims under the rules and regulations framed under the 1909 Council's Act. Sapru had a natural dislike for separate representation. But he agreed to it simply for the sake of a compromise. As we shall see later compromise was the most important element of his political faith. "I believe in the moral influence of compromise..." Throughout his whole political life he worked for this compromise—compromise between the Hindus and the Muslims, between the Government and the Congress. That he did not achieve a conspicuous success is no reflection either on his faith or on himself.

Sapru's political philosophy evolved with his growing age and maturity. Also owing to newer challenges coming up, he was more concerned with the super-structure of democracy like the federation idea which he tried hard to make acceptable. But initially his sympathy appears to have been for the village panchayat system. Sapru supported a resolution in the U.P. Council which recommended the formation of village panchayats empowered to settle petty cases and to carry on local self-governing duties. His only point was that the experiment should be carried on with a little caution. He cogently argued that there was representation from the Imperial Council down to the Municipal Board but none below that. But it was the village life which was the unit of public work or ought to be, and "it is this unit which is absolutely unrepresented and absolutely undeveloped"[20] he emphasised. This early sympathy for the traditional rural policy appears to have made it easy for him to collaborate with Dr. Annie Besant in framing the Commonwealth of India Bill in which the panchayat system was made the base of the democratic structure.

After the Surat split the Moderates seized the initiative. By adopting a new Congress constitution at Madras in 1908, the Moderates barred the door to extremism in any form. The 1909 Reforms as well as the annulment of the partition of Bengal yielded them some political dividends so as to ensure their safe continuance in command of the organisation. Besides, the Government's severe repressive measures involving the incarceration of leaders like Tilak went on unabated, driving extremism down, though only for the time being. Subsequently as the world war started, the Moderates burst out in an effusion of loyalty to the British crown.

The most disquieting aspect of the situation, namely, the spread of the cult of the bomb and the pistol, was however continuing. Revolutionary activities were being attempted in several parts of the country, and even from foreign soil. That such activities were not deterred by the outbreak of the world war would be as evident from such incidents as the emergence of the Ghadar Party in America and others. The Government resorted to the most rigorous repression, enacted drastic laws and clamped down severe restrictions on the people. The formation of the Rowlatt Committee, the repressive laws coming in its wake and the great tragedy at Jallianwallah Bagh are too well known to need reiteration. They might have been calm on the surface but the country's mood was really sullen. The Moderates were trying desperately to hold their own against the rising tempo of public discontent but not very successfully. In 1916 there was a temporary Moderate Extremist entente through the good offices, among others, of Mrs. Annie Besant. But things were tending towards more startling developments.

Tilak returned to active politics in 1914. That made for a change in the situation which warmed up further when Mrs. Annie Besant left behind her theosophical isolation to plunge headlong into politics. She herself facilitated the Extremist re-entry into the Congress fold. But this uneasy union received a rude jolt when Mrs. Besant was elected to preside over the 1917 Congress, much to the chagrin of the elder leadership. It virtually became a Congress of Mrs. Besant and Tilak, marking the point of no return in the Moderate Extremist cleavage. In 1918 the Moderates formed their own National Liberal Federation which Sapru necessarily joined.

The Home Rule Movement initiated by Tilak and Mrs. Besant at a short interval brought a new animation into the comparatively sluggish political scene. The movement could not be called Extremist in any particular way but did have a more radical edge than the placid politics of the Moderates. For a time it created a broad forum for various schools of political thought to come together. Some Moderates of course joined it. But on the whole it seems to have widened the gulf. Veteran Surendra Nath Bannerjee says that the Home Rule Movement created a division in the Congress.[21]

Despite his characteristic moderation and strict constitutional upbringing, Sapru was more forward looking than many other leaders of his school. Else, he would not have been so easily drawn towards the Home Rule image. Deeply impressed by Mrs. Besant's personality and politics, Sapru along with Motilal Nehru strongly protested when that remarkable lady, who had breathed a new life into the country's national scene, was put under arrest in 1917. Needless to say, both Sapru and Motilal joined the Home Rule Movement.

What indeed is the nature of Indian liberalism? "Indian liberalism is the product of European liberalism. The Indian intellectuals have almost literally sat at the feet of the English liberals and drawn inspiration from them ... Give us democracy, they said, give us the same parliamentary institutions you Englishmen enjoy, and we will do the same wonderful things which you did...Indian history to them was an extension of English history; Indian politics was a further development of English politics."[22] That might have been the way liberalism began. But there is much to be said in favour of the Liberals. Inspite of their being English oriented, they were neither upstarts nor un-Indian but were sturdy patriots and vigorous fighters for their country's cause. The liberal creed was moulded by the historical circumstances and psychological millieu of that age. At a time when Indian nationalism had started taking timid strides, no other creed or political methodology was possible than the Liberals had adopted. Having been deeply immersed in English political and constitutional history, they naturally accepted the British parliamentary system to be the best under the circumstances and developed an implicit faith in the British intentions and professions. But when they were disappointed they did not hesitate to speak out and even non-cooperated, as will be seen later from Sapru's and several other liberal leaders' attitude towards the Simon Commission. They tried persistently, of course in their own constructive way, to advance the political interests of their country and never shrank back under any circumstances. Of course they believed in the beneficial effect of the British rule on India and their political ambition was confined to self-government within the Empire.

On its birth in Bombay under the Presidentship of Surendra Nath Bannerjee, the National Liberal Federation said that "we the Liberal party are the friends of evolution and enemies of revolution", and that it would cooperate when it could and criticize when it must.[22]

The Liberals were firmly opposed to non-cooperation and believed in an evolutionary way of constitutional progress admitting of a process of gradualness. That is why they welcomed Montagu proposals as a significant advance towards their objective and indeed it was their acceptance of the proposals which in a large measure encouraged Montagu to go ahead with his scheme. That they did this as strategy for gaining more would be evident from the later events. Noticeably, even some Congressmen also favoured this strategy.

Meanwhile India had made an impressive contribution to Britain's war efforts and at a considerable sacrifice of men, money and materials. To give an instance, there were at the start of the war some 80,000 British officers and men and some 230,000 Indian ranks. But as the war progressed the Government recruited over 800,000 combatants and over 400,000 non-combatants.[22] The Indians had to put up with the high handedness of the British recruiting and war fund collecting agencies and also suffer severe abridgment of civil liberty on account of the Defence of India Rules. In addition, they had to face an acute economic crisis.

India's sincere and significant contribution to the war efforts emboldened the people to look forward to, and indeed to demand, substantial constitutional advance in keeping with the national objective. Even the Moderates felt encouraged to do so. On the whole, "the politically minded classes steadfastly set before their eyes the aim of asserting India's right to attain a place among the Self-Governing Dominions of the British Commonwealth".[22] The ideal of responsible government within the Empire came to the forefront in political discussions as never before and afforded a stimulus to constructive constitutional activities".[23]

Constitutional efforts on the part of the Indians were made in the shape of the Memorandum of 19 to which Sapru was a signatory and the Congress League scheme, both in 1916. In these formulations Sapru was playing his own quiet role. When the Congress League scheme, representing the nearest political consensus of the two parallel parties, was put in the form of a resolution at the 1916 Lucknow Congress by Surendra Nath Bannerjee, Sapru was one of the persons who rose to support it. Finally came the Montagu Chelmsford Reforms which the Moderates accepted and agreed to work for whatever they might have been worth. During this period Sapru was functioning first in the U.P. Legislative Council and then in the Indian Legislative Council. Sapru was at his best in the houses of legislature. He was not a leader who could shine among the crowd on the street or on the platform.

Sapru was sworn in as a member of the Indian Legislative Council in September, 1916, and easily became one of the stalwarts of the house. His keen analytical mind and his vast knowledge of political affairs at once marked him out as a parliamentarian of a very high order. He never ceased to plead passionately for any measure which he considered good for his country. As already noted, education was a subject very dear to his heart and as he pleaded for educational expansion for his home province in the U.P. Legislative Council, so did he do for the country as a whole in the Indian Legislative Council. As early as in 1917, he had the courage and vision to urge the authorities to undertake such bold measures of reform as the introduction of universal free compulsory education within 15 years.[24]

India's increasing share in the defence of the country was another pet subject of his, for which he pleaded fervently on many forums and on many occasions. This was because he felt that a country that aspired to self rule must first of all be capable of self-defence. Thus, when the Commander in Chief introduced a bill in the Council for building up an auxiliary force, Sapru supported it not only as a war measure but also as an evidence of the Government's decreasing distrust of the Indians in defence matters. Calling for an absolute equality of rank, position and opportunity for the Indians in the army, he said: "We take our stand on our birth-right, our privilege, that we shall be admitted to the same position as Europeans are in the army..."[25]

Owing to India's significant contribution to war efforts and the appreciation of the same by prominent British statesmen, there was legitimate expectation in the country that the end of the war would see liberal constitutional reforms being granted. On his assumption of office in 1916, Lord Chelmsford is said to have spoken in similar tones at the first meeting of the Executive Council.[26] However, a very timid type of Government of India despatch was sent to the Secretary of State. But even this failed to evoke response. Subsequently, the newly appointed Secretary of State, Montagu came personally to study the situation in this country.

During the discussion on the budget for 1917-18 in the Legislative Council, Sapru made the point that the people should be given an opportunity to express themselves on the reform proposals which had till then been kept a closely guarded secret.

The publication of the Montague-Chelmsford proposals raised a storm of controversy, both mild and virulent in different quarters. Describing the proposals as "substantial steps", Chelmsford said in the Legislative Council on September 4, 1918: "Criticize them freely. But remember that if your criticism is to be useful it must be constructive and not merely destructive". The Viceroy was looking for Moderate support and it came soon enough. In a resolution moved in the House on September 7, 1918, Surendra Nath Bannerjee supported the proposals and at the same time suggested the formation of a committee of all the non-official members of the Council to examine and make recommendations on the proposals. Supporting the resolution Sapru said that the Reform proposals "are a genuine effort and they do constitute a definite advance towards responsible government in India."[27]

Sumning up the reforms, Sapru observed that local self-government complete power and in provincial self-government partial power was to be handed over, while in the Central Government the Indian sphere of influence was to be enlarged. Further in the Provincial Government, the Legislative machinery was to be overhauled with certain subjects being transferred to popular Ministers who would thus be vested with an element of responsibility. He was critical of certain points. For example, he was not satisfied with the adjustment of finances between the transferred and the reserved subjects. He also wanted an element of responsibility at the Centre and a larger elected majority. Yet he felt that sixty seven elected members out of the 100 constituting the Central Council is "a substantial majority". In this way giving the support expected of the Moderates to the proposals, Sapru said that if Sir Sankaran Nair, Bhupen Basu, Surendra Nath Bannerjee and Wacha, who had endorsed the proposed reforms scheme, were not "patriots" but "traitors" to the cause, he was willing "to stand in the same dock with them."[28]

Sapru rose to his highest stature as a parliamentarian, as a statesman and above all as a patriot during the debate in the Indian Legislative Council on the two Rowlatt bills. These were the British Government's two precious gifts in return for India's loyalty to, and sacrifice for, the allied cause. And they came at a time when the country's high expectations about reform proposals had been thoroughly belied. These two bills also exposed the traditionally double faced India policy of the British Government. No wonder the country was thrown into a convulsion of anguish and anger by the introduction of the two bills which also, signalized the starting of *satyagraha* by Gandhiji and the chain of events claiming in the Jallianwallah Bagh tragedy.

Intervening in the debate on the Criminal Law (Emergency Powers) Bill, Sapru said: "My Lord, if it is not undiluted coercion, I ask what is it in all humility?"[29] These stringent words uttered more than half a century ago would still ring in the ears of Sapru's countrymen. These were the words of a man labelled Moderate but having the stoutest heart of a patriot and an unflinching love for liberty. Declaring that "it is our duty to oppose the Bill", he tore to shreds the argument that those who did not support the Bill had a soft corner for anarchism, and said that the Bill would fail because anarchist violence could not be cured by that sort of measure which the Government had tried during the previous decade without success.

In opposing the Bill, he put forward powerful arguments saying, among other things, that the Bill was inopportune at that crucial moment of the country's history. He said: "...I have no hesitation in saying that it is wholly wrong in principle, unsound in its conception, dangerous in its operation and too sweeping and too comprehensive, indeed far more comprehensive than many of us are prepared to admit at the present moment".[30] He further said: "... as a lawyer trained in the British system of jurisprudence, as an Indian who loves his country and who is interested in the orderly progress of his country, who wants self-government, who is anxious to have responsible government at an early date and who is anxious for permanent connection between India and England, my Lord, I think it is my duty to oppose the measure".[31] Like, a prophet he foresaw "the whirlpool of agitation" into which the Bill was going to throw the country and warned the Government against it.

The Bill sought to invest the Executive with large arbitrary powers uncontrolled by the Judiciary and it was easy to see that there was tension and excitement over the Bill among men of all shades of opinion and politicians of all schools. Sapru could easily foresee that the Bill meant to supplement the ordinary criminal law and confer Emergency powers on the Executive was bound to add fuel to the fire of the smouldering public discontent. He therefore made a vigorous effort to stop the Bill, at least to postpone it.

While the first Bill was in the nature of emergency provisions for a temporary period, the second one, that is, the Criminal Law (Amendment) Bill provided for permanent changes in the country's ordinary criminal law, and was introduced in the Council on February 10, 1919. Sapru opposed the Bill as strongly as he did the first one and suggested the circulation of the Bill for eliciting public opinion and the opinion of the High Courts and the Local Governments. The Bill sought to make punishable the possession of seditious documents unless the possessor could prove them for lawful purposes. Sapru gave an interesting example saying that since the Home Member was daily bringing seditious documents to the Council chamber to read out from, he could be presumed to be coming within the mischief of the Bill, unless he proved them to be for lawful purpose, and the members affirmed this. Speaking thus in a humorous vein Sapru exposed the absurdity of the provisions of the Bill and thus turned the tables on the honourable Home Member.[32]

Yet good sense did not dawn upon the ruling authorities. Persuasions failed. Warnings were not heeded. They went ahead with the two Bills thinking that they could suppress an awakened nation with those rigorous enactments. The chain of events resulting from the passage of the Bills is well-known. The entire country was thrown into the vortex of an unprecedented unrest. Its political profile was completely radicalized.

Sapru was not a kowtow Moderate. He did not timidly follow in the footsteps of the official bosses. He accepted the Reforms, no doubt. But he was a strong dissenter where necessary and never failed to speak out in his country's interest regardless of official displeasure.

One thing more, Sapru's spectacular performance in the Indian Legislative Council marked him out as a leader of an all India stature.

REFERENCES

1. Sitaramayya, P., *History of the Congress, 1885 to 1936* (Bombay: Padama Publications), 1948.
2. Raina, K.N. and K.V. Gopala Ratnam, *Recollections and Impressions, op. cit.*
3. Parvate, T.V., *Gopal Krishna Gokhale* (Ahmedabad: Navajivan Publishing House), 1959.
4. Mathur, B.D., *Gokhale—A Political Biography* (Bombay: Himalaya Publishers), 1955.
5. Besant Annie, *How India Wrought for Freedom: The Story of Indian National Congress* (New Delhi: Michiko Panjathan), 1975.
6. Chintamani, C.Y., "The Provincial Conferences of Allahabad", *Modern Review*, May 1907.
7. Chintamani, C.Y., *Indian Politics Since Mutiny* (Allahabad: Kitabistan), 1947.
8. Besant Annie, *How India Wrought for Freedom, op cit.*
9. *Report, Indian National Congress, 1910.*
10. *Ibid.*, 1916.
11. P.N. Sapru, 'Some Memories of My Father', in Raina and Gopala (eds.), *Tej Bahadur Sapru: Profiles and Tributes, op. cit.*, p. 63.
12. Raina (ed.), *Tej Bahadur Sapru —Responsa: Selected Legal Opinions, op. cit.*, pp. vii-viii.
13. Hindustan Review Enters its Fiftieth Year, *Hindustan Review*, July 1949.
14. Chintamani, C.Y., *Indian Politics Since Mutiny, op. cit.*
15. Dutt, Iswara K., *The Street of Ink* (London: John Arden), 1955.
16. U.P. Legislative Council Proceedings, 1916.

17. *Ibid.*, 1915.
18. *Ibid.*
19. *Ibid.*
20. *Ibid.*
21. Bannerjee, S.N., *A Nation in Making* (London: Milford), 1925.
22. Buch, M.A., *The Rise and Growth of Indian Liberalism* (Baroda: the auth), 1938.
23. Shukla, B.D., *History of the Indian Liberal Party* (Calcutta: Bharti Publishers), 1957.
24. Williams Rushbrook, L.F., *India in the Years 1917-18* (Gladwin: Francis), 1975.
25. *Ibid.*
26. *Ibid.*
27. *Indian Legislative Council Proceedings, February* 2, 1917.
28. *Ibid.*, February 21, 1917.
29. Setalvad, C.H., *Recollections and Reflections* (Bombay: Padama), 1946.
30. *Indian Legislative Council Proceedings, September* 7, 1918.
31. *Ibid.*
32. *Ibid.*, February 7, 1919.
33. *Ibid.*
34. *Ibid.*
35. *Ibid.*, February 10, 1919.

3

THE FEDERAL CONCEPT

Sir Tej Bahadur Sapru was a statesman whose place in the pantheon of India's modern history is assured beyond doubt. Statesman and jurist, he was in his day the embodiment of Liberalism. With him Liberalism represented an unwavering adherence to national liberty, and to the freedom of the individual, though his view of these great ideals may have been circumscribed by his legal and constitutional training. Revolutionary ideas and mass movements did not arouse any sympathy in him. Political action appeared to his essentially rational mind, a matter for argument and negotiation. It is in an atmosphere of argument and debate that he showed. The Round Table Conference held in London in the years 1930-33 provided him a great opportunity. It would not be too much to say that from the beginning to the end his personality dominated the scene in St. James' Palace. The federal scheme which, with modification, Free India accepted as her own was mainly his work.[1]

The First Round Table Conference which was inaugurated in London on November 12, 1930, and was presided over by Prime Minister Ramsay MacDonald had an unpropitious start. It began in the depressing climate of Congress rejection, countrywide unrest and an unsolved communal tangle. The issue before it was as to what would be the next step in India's constitutional progress. But the most vital element in India's political life, namely, the Congress, was not there, while the most essential ingredient of such a progress, namely, communal settlement, was a far cry.

The invitees to the Conference were the Liberals (not sympathetic to non-cooperation), representatives of the Sikhs, the

Muslims, the Depressed Classes, and those of commercial and industrial interests and European delegates from the Indian States. The list of invitees was carefully made as if to advertise the fragmented nature of India's political life rather than its basic unity. The choice of the Muslim delegates was made in such a manner as to exclude any nationalist element, and it is believed to have been influenced by the Viceroy's Executive Councillor Fazli Hussain. It is no wonder therefore that the Muslim delegates *en masse* demanded "adequate" safeguards for their community as a pre-condition to any constitutional settlement.

Yet in many ways it was a memorable conference where the Indian and the British delegates for the first time sat across the table on a plane of equality to settle constitutional issues. The Indian members were united in their demand for an early transfer of responsibility to the Indian hands, even subject to transitional safeguards. But of course the British representatives including even those belonging to the Labour Party were not ready to concede so much and so soon.

More than Dominion Status which to the Indian delegates was the main theme of the RTC, a new idea, that of an all-India federation, emerged on the Conference horizon and took it by storm, as it were. Vaguely hinted at by the Simon Commission and officially considered rather nebulous till then, the conception of an Indian federation comprising both the Indian States and the Provinces assumed for the first time the shape of a concrete political proposition claiming a considerable part of the delegates' attention. Sapru who came out as India's most eloquent spokesman sponsored the federation idea with an extraordinary passion and fervour.

No other Indian spokesman could perhaps measure up to the stature Sapru rose to, while opening his country's case before the Conference. On November 17, he made a remarkable speech which has become historic since then. In the absence of the Congress he spoke on behalf of India as a whole, not for any section or segment of it, urging the British to take a broad statesmanlike view of the Indian problem and appealed to the Princes to join in the all-India federation. He called upon the British rulers to take note of the seething unrest which he and his friend Jayakar had witnessed during their wide tours in the country and asked them to disabuse their minds that the Indians vibrating with a new life would remain content with their present position. The impact of his speech was tremendous. "Tej Bahadur Sapru who initiated the discussion on November 17 created a sensation by his remarkable speech which changed the whole atmosphere of the Conference."[2] The salient points of Sapru's speech were these: First, he urged the British rulers to take a statesmanlike view of the Indian situation. Secondly, he exposed the utter absurdity of the British continuing to rule 320 million people from the seat of their political authority, 6,000 miles away. British sovereignty over India came down, in his opinion, to half a dozen men in England and half a dozen men in India. Thirdly, he asserted India's right to seek freedom saying "... it is perfectly natural that we seek freedom, freedom within our borders as an integral part of the British Commonwealth of Nations". In short, he demanded Dominion Status on a footing of equality having a government "not merely responsive but responsible to the popular voice."[3]

Sapru's solution to the Indian problem was federation. He said "... I am a strong believer in the federal form of government. I believe that therein lies the solution of difficulty and the salvation of India. ..."[4] His passionate appeal to the Princes was a masterpiece of Oratory. He was burning with the fire of patriotism and zeal for national unity. He told the Princes: "Let me respectfully tell them that they are Indians first and Indian Princes next and that they owe as much duty to the common motherland as we do... I ask them (the Princes) to say whether at any time in history, India was so arbitrarily divided geographically—British and Indian India. I say we are one India. Let them move forward with the vision of an India which will be one single whole, each part of which will be autonomous and may enjoy absolute independence within its borders, regulated by proper relations with the rest. Therefore I ask them to come forth on this occasion and say whether they are prepared to join an all India federation".[5]

What sort of a federation would it be? Where would the residuary powers lie with the Centre or with the Provinces? What would be the Princes' relation with the Centre? What would happen to their treaty rights? These and other complicated matters had to be thrashed out to give form and content to this still indeterminate idea. But the Princes' acceptance must be there, first and foremost. Originally Sapru had been in favour of the residuary powers vested in the Centre. But for the sake of communal amity and a united India he seems gradually to have modified his views in favour of a federation with the residuary powers vested in the units. In the present case the Princes would surely not agree to federate unless the absolute internal autonomy of the federating units, at any rate of their States, was guaranteed. On behalf of the Princes the Maharaja of Bikaner responded well, saying, "We of the Indian States are willing to take our part in, and make our contribution, to the greater prosperity and contentment of India as a whole. I am convinced that we can best make that contribution through a federal system of government composed of the States and British India".[6] This however was subject to the States, as well as their subjects, rights and interests being safeguarded. Personally the Maharaja did not like the 'two Indias' theory.

In any federal scheme the Princes would naturally be anxious to safeguard their own rights and interests and to be assured of freedom from interference in their internal affairs. Many Princes grew suspicious of the federal idea and eventually cooled down. Chimanlal Setalvad analyses the Princes motives thus.[7] They might have been wanting to be free from the interference of the Political Department without however entrusting all their rights and interests to the keeping of a federal government dominated by the British Indians. They would therefore have their treaty rights outside the jurisdiction of the federal government. Whatever the motive might have been, their initial response gave some substance to the grand design and encouraged hopes of its fulfilment in future. Federation thus became the main framework of the subsequent reforms scheme, though not implemented owing to the Princes' later reluctance.

After the plenary session, the Conference divided itself into several committees to work out the details. The Federal Structure Committee framed a federation Scheme, other committees made a number of recommendations, for example, the abolition of Dyarchy. These committees worked well and produced good results which were discussed at the Conference. But it was in the Minorities Committee that the deadlock occurred. In that it was agreed on principle that the proposed new constitution must assure the minorities that their interests would be safeguarded. Beyond this it was found difficult to make any headway. The Muslims and the Sikhs demanded safeguards. Even the Depressed Classes asserted their separate electoral identity. The Muslim delegates insisted that no constitutional advance was possible or practicable at the Centre or in the Provinces without adequate safeguards for the Muslims. Of course they were the best judge of what "adequate" was. The Conference reached a dead end.

In this connection an incident having a bearing on the Muslim attitude deserves a brief mention. Setalvad tells the story of how on the eve of the Conference, the Hindu and Muslim leaders used to meet at the Nawab of Bhopal's residence to hammer out a solution. Leader of the Muslims, Aga Khan agreed to joint electorates with reservation of seats for the Muslims and also to supporting the national demand at the Conference provided his other demands were met. These demands were the reconstitution of Sind and NWFP as separate provinces, reasonable weightage for the Muslims in the provinces and one-third representation for them at the Centre. (Incidentally, the idea of federation had not come up till then). Setalvad says that Sapru, Shastri and he himself would have readily agreed but for the fact that Moonie and Javakar demurred. Meanwhile reactionary elements in India and London started pressuring the Muslim delegation and the latter's attitude stiffened with the result that the situation got out of the Aga Khan's hands.[8]

From Fazli Husain's biography by his son Azim Husain, it is known that the former got the scert of what was going on in London and rebuked the Muslim delegation for their liberal leanings. From India he manoeuvred things in such a way that from that time onwards the Muslim delegates of all shades of opinion started insisting on their 'safeguards demand' being met as a condition precedent to any communal settlement, and the joint electorates idea thus got scuttled. It was about this time that Iqbal and a little later Rahmat Ali propounded their Muslim nation thesis. It also appears that the Muslim delegates to the conference were getting in touch with the British opposition leaders, that is, the Conservative British politicians with a view to stalling any settlement except on their own terms. The well meaning efforts of the Labour Government, particularly of Secretary of State Benn, was thus frustrated and the Minorities Committee left the communal question unsolved.

A man of indefatigable courage and optimism, Sapru went on pleading for communal settlement and for taking a broad nationalistic view of the problem. During discussion on the Federal Structure Committee's report, both Jinnah and Shafi insisted on communal safeguards as a condition precedent to the working of any constitution to be framed. Replying, Sapru said that while he was in complete sympathy with the Muslim demand for safeguards, there were at the same time millions of Hindus and Muslims who wanted an honourable settlement and the issue had to be settled in the larger interests of the country. Speaking strongly against sectional outlook, he urged the delegates to demonstrate that "where the interests of the country are concerned, we are prepared to make any sacrifice of our prejudices and predilections", and expressed the hope that the communal problem would be settled at any early date.[9] But Sapru was hoping against hope. From the beginning, the conference trend was running counter to his optimism which naturally went unrewarded. "There are some in the conference who would care to place the communal interests above the interests of the nation as a whole. They would not care to wait for a free India to make the necessary communal adjustments. Communal adjustments were therefore conditions precedent to their co-operating in any scheme of responsible national government in India. Either Jinnah's 14 points or none of any responsible constitution devoid of British control—these were the only possible alternatives present in their thoughts."[10]

In his summing up speech the Prime Minister made the following major points: (a) The Government's view was that responsibility should be placed upon the Legislature both Central and Provincial, subject to certain safeguards; (b) The Government to took note of the unanimous recommendation about federation; and (c) Regarding the minorities problem "it was the duty of the communities to come to an agreement among themselves". Lastly, he expressed the hope that those engaged in civil disobedience would respond to the Viceroy's appeal (made in the Central Assembly on January 17, 1931) and thus turn their attention to co-operative work.[11]

Despite contrary opinion in other quarters, Sapru felt satisfied that the Conference had not gone in vain. In his opinion, it had broken new grounds in three respects: responsibility at the Centre, All India Federation, and Indian preparation for self-defence. Unlike many others he was not at all bothered about the safeguards for the transitional period. These, he felt, were in India's own interest.

The Viceroy's conciliatory speech in the Central Legislature on January 17, 1931, followed by the Prime Minister's concluding address at the RTC indicated that the Government might have realized the futility of a conference without the Congress and was perhaps keen on its participation. They were thus getting ready to make a conciliatory gesture. Here was one more opportunity for Sapru and his colleagues to review their mediating efforts so that the Congress might sit at the next RTC. While Sapru and his colleagues were working studiously to that end, the Government gave the signal for a possible end of confrontation by releasing Gandhiji and the Working Committee members on January 26, 1931, even before the RTC delegates had returned home. The Working Committee reacted sharply to the RTC decision as well as the Prime Minister's speech on the ground that they fell far short of the Congress demand, but some of the Moderate leaders wired Gandhiji requesting the Congress to suspend judgment until they came back and discussed the matter with the leaders. On their return they had prolonged discussions with the Working Committee early in February, at Allahabad. "For a few weeks Moderate influences at the Anand Bhawan tried their level best to soften and knead the attitude of the Congress to the requisite degree of plasticity. Sapru, Jayakar and Shastri all excelled themselves in the art of pleading and persuasion. But the wide cleavage between the RTC point of view and that of the Congress could not be easily narrowed or cemented."[12] Meanwhile Gandhiji was corresponding with the Viceroy without much of an encouraging result, initially. At last it was arranged that he would meet the Viceroy at the latter's invitation. Sapru and his colleagues' earnest mediation efforts did not go in vain. They initiated a process of rapprochement which ultimately led to the signing of the Gandhi-Irwin Pact. During the Mahatma's prolonged parleys with the Viceroy from February 17 to March 5, 1931, on which day the Pact was signed, Sapru was kept constantly informed of the proceedings. On Februarv 27, the Viceroy asked him and Jayakar to be present at the talks.[13] The following day he forwarded to Sapru the copy of a letter he had written to Gandhiji, detailing several points to be incorporated in the agreement, like an effective withdrawal of the civil disobedience movement, withdrawal of the ordinances, release of prisoners and so on.[14] Sapru and Jayakar played their part well enough so as to induce the Congress and the Government to end confrontation and sit across the table. Though committed to complete independence, the Congress agreed to join the RTC on the basis of the points thrashed out at the first conference federation, Indian responsibility with safeguards and protection for the minorities' interests. Gandhiji was appointed the sole Congress representative at the Conference. The line of thinking advocated by Sapru and his friends triumphed for the time being.

All this synchronized with big and ominous changes in England and in India. Lord Willingdon replaced Irwin in India in April 1931, and a Conservative dominated national government took the place of the earlier Labour administration with Sir Samuel Hoare as the Secretary of State for India. The spirit of 'Irwinism' which paved the way for a possible Congress participation in the RTC was clearly over and diehardism was once again revived. A glimpse of the new emerging situation consequent upon Willingdon's arrival in India can be had from Jayakar's to Sapru: "I see signs that the forces against 'Sapru Jayakar influence'...are strengthening, and I should not be surprised if at the vital stages of further work in India about the RTC we find it difficult to have our views respected to the same extent that Lord Irwin did.[15] Sapru was insistent on Gandhiji's going to England and requested Jayakar to persuade him to do so. Sapru wrote to Jayakar: "... I think he can do a good deal by his visit to England and by adopting a reasonable attitude."[16] Jayakar who was even hopeful about Gandhiji joining the RTC wrote to Sapru: "...it is our plain duty to keep as near Gandhi as we can..."[17]

Gandhiji himself was however not so optimistic. His two vital propositions, agreed basis for Dominion Status and Communal settlement were nowhere in sight. The communal problem had in particular become intractable. The Congress communal settlement scheme of July 1931 had evoked no response, and Gandhiji's own efforts at home had failed. Would they fare better in England at the conference table? "The Muslims no longer, thought of themselves as a minority but as a nationality".[18]

The curtain was rung up again in London where the second Act of the Round Table Conference drama commenced on September 7, 1931, with even leaner chances of success than on the first occasion. With the change of Government in England the Conservatives had virtually captured power under the Labourite Prime Ministership, of a much weakened Ramsay MacDonald. That official attitude which desired Congress participation in the Conference, and even went a long way to meet the Congress point of view to secure its participation in the Conference was no more. With the overt and covert support of the Conservative elements in England and the European community resident in India, Muslim separation had also got greatly strengthened as a factor in any political settlement. Then there were Depressed Classes who raised varying lines of separation so as to criss-cross the scene beyond redemption. The chorus of discordant voices only tended to show that India was not a nation but a conglomeration of different and often conflicting nationalities and religious groups. This is exactly what the conservatives were manoeuvering to show up. There was another straw in the wind. The British politicians did not seem inclined to concede anything beyond what the Simon Commission had reported. The Labour Party itself did not seem to be willing to go far enough. To hark back to the Simon Commission at that stage when the RTC had generated so much hope and expectation was like putting the clock back.

The Conference went straight to brass tacks by activating the Federal Structure Committee (FSC) and the Minorities Committee (MC). As sole Congress representative, Gandhiji was a member of both. It was his main endeavour to persuade the Conference that the Congress was not a sectarian organization but a national one representing all sections of the people and all communities. He strongly objected to the separatist demand by the Scheduled Castes. He would concede separate electorates to the Muslims and the Sikhs but not to the Scheduled Castes. He had prolonged discussions with Jinnah and other minority leaders. In fact the meetings of the Minorities Committee were postponed to facilitate these discussions. These efforts however proved futile.

On the political plane, Gandhiji's main demand was for the immediate establishment of responsible government in the Provinces and at the Centre with full control over the Army, Defence and External Affairs. An Army controlled by an alien government was an army of occupation, he said. But his passionate pleadings were of no avail. Gandhiji came back to India a frustrated man.

Nothing was more painful for Sapru than that Gandhiji's presence should go for nothing, specially because he felt a sense of personal involvement in ensuring Gandhiji's participation. He worked untiringly at the Conference table and in private discussions and tried to strengthen Gandhiji's position, despite differences with him on many matters. Sapru paid a tribute to Gandhiji, saying that he was one man for whom the freedom of India did not mean freedom for this section or that, but freedom for every body.

At the FSC meetings Sapru made valuable contributions to the filling up of the details of the federal scheme. On all controversial issues Sapru followed a line of compromise knowing full well that any radical demand was bound to be rejected. Since the British would not like to hand over the Army and Defence, Sapru suggested a via media at the FSC—an Indian member in charge of the Army portfolio appointed by the Governor-General and associated with the Defence matters side by side with supremacy of the Commander-in-Chief appointed by the Crown in technical matters. This was Sapru's compromise formula. He did not let go the opportunity to voice his favourite demand for the Indianization of the Army. In this connection he urged and rightly so, the abolition of the artificial distinction between the martial and the non-martial races and pleaded for throwing open the ranks of the Army to all classes of people. He said: "This division of the population of India into martial and non-martial is an arbitrary division, which has arisen owing to the political exigencies of the last fifty or sixty years, and I see no reason why any man of any caste or religion should be debarred from entering the Army, provided he satisfies the necessary conditions required for an Army career.[19]

Similarly on External Affairs, Sapru's compromise formula was that, while matters relating to peace and war should belong exclusively to the jurisdiction of the Governor-General, many other matters generally treated as external but actually affecting the commercial and other aspects of the country should be within the Indian Legislative competence.

The totality of Sapru's views can be gathered from his speech at the plenary session on November 30, 1931. First, he affirmed that "the idea of an all India federation presenting as it does, the prospect of many centuries of a United India with all its defects and all its shortcomings, is the only idea on which we can work.[20] Secondly, as if he could read the British mind which was then tending towards the Simon Commission report and provincial autonomy, he strongly opposed the idea and demanded a comprehensive scheme covering both the Centre and the Provinces.

Regarding the Princes joining the federation, he was anxious that they should do so if necessary on their own terms. This to his mind was the basic step towards building up the united India of his dream. Once they federated, their relations with the Centre and the other units were bound to undergo transformation, depending on the political circumstances. Sapru was in favour of direct election to the Central Lower House, but the States might be left to devise their own method. While conceding this, he urged the Princes to give their subjects a voice in the election to the Lower House. Apparently he did not want to force the hands of the Princes; since that might spoil the prospects of the federation. But with his remarkable foresight he could visualize the day when the Princes would be induced to satisfy the aspirations of their subjects.

On the communal question he told the plenary session that there was no sacrifice not worth making in winning over the minorities and would not himself quarrel over any measure of settlement as long as the settlement was there. But the disputed issues must be settled by the Indians themselves. In default the

Government might take the matter in its own hand. This was an anticipation of the Communal Award which was not long delayed.

At the final session on December 1, 1931, the Prime Minister restated the Government policy which in substance was the grant of responsibility to the Centre and the Provinces subject to certain transitional safeguards and the protection of the minorities' rights and interests together with the recognition of the idea of an All India Federation. There was however an ominous ring in his incidental observation that while federation was a complicated process, provincial autonomy was much simpler.[21] Apparently the Government's mind was still moving within the narrow groove of provincial autonomy which had been tried and found wanting. Lastly, the Prime Minister sounded equally ominous when he hinted, as already anticipated by Sapru, that if the Conference failed to arrive at a communal settlement, the Government might have to frame and supply one.[22] Three Committees were proposed to go into the questions of federation, finance and franchise. Another committee was to function in India as a Consultative Committee or the Working Committee of the Conference. This indicated that the Conference method was a continuing process. Sapru was made a member of the Consultative Committee.

The Second RTC thus came to a close. Prolonged discussions were held on such questions as the modalities of framing a constitutional structure, the composition of the federal legislature, mode of accession, distribution of finances and others. Certain majority opinions were recorded. But on the whole there was not much progress. Worst of all, the communal question remained dangerously unsettled.

Sapru would not have reforms by piecemeal. He would oppose any idea of having the Provincial part of the constitution implemented while leaving the Centre untouched. But his efforts supported by many others, were being checkmated almost at every step. Apart from the unsolved communal tangle there was another retarding factor. The right-wing British politicians then dominating the Government had apparently no intention of conceding anything beyond the Simon recommendations. In this reactionary design they had their allies in the Europeans settled in India, among others. If the Muslim attitude had stiffened beyond all reasonable limits, it was largely owing to British right wing encouragement.

When Gandhi returned to India a thoroughly frustrated man, the whole country was afire. The Government of the new Viceroy Willingdon had relegated the Gandhi-Irwin Pact to scrap heap and a rigorous Ordinance Raj had been ushered in, accompanied by unrelenting repression. U.P. was passing through a great agrarian upheaval with Jawaharlal Nehru playing the leading part in it. The North-Western Frontier Province had become a stir with the Khudai Khidmatgar Movement led by the Khan Brothers. Bengal was having a recrudescence of the bomb and pistol cult. In vain did Gandhiji seek an interview with an unbending Viceroy. Before long Gandhiji was in jail.

Towards the end of June 1932, the intentions of the National Government in Britain became more clear. The Tories in England were no longer ready to share constitution making with the Indians, and Sir Samuel Hoare was anxious to wriggle out of the commitment. Labour had driven him into. Hoare's announcement in the House of Commons on June 27, 1932, foreshadowed the coming of the Communal Award. At the same time, he proposed the substitution of the RTC method by a Joint Select Committee of Parliament going ahead with the constitution making for India. The RTC presupposed equal membership of the Indians with the British at the conference table. But the Joint Select Committee meant that the Indians could only appear before it as witnesses or at best hold private discussions with it. This abrupt change in procedure went wholly against the strategy to which Irwin had solemnly committed himself. Naturally, there were strong protests in India, particularly from the Liberals. It was surprising that, while the RTC method itself was being jettisoned, its Working Committee in India, of which Sapru was a member, was expected to carry on its labours for formulating proposals to be placed before the Joint Select Committee. In a statement issued on June 29, 1932, Sapru and Jayakar expressed grave dissatisfaction over this new arrangement. Regarding the single bill proposed by the Secretary of State covering both the Centre and the federating units, they warned that the principle of voluntary federation which might be conceded to the States because of their special circumstances, could not however be granted to the Provinces, because in that case a single recalcitrant Province might hold up the federation indefinitely.[23]

In protest against the change of policy, Sapru, Joshi and Jayakar resigned from the Consultative Committee. Sapru strongly felt that the change was not only of the mode but of substance and spirit. At a meeting of some RTC delegates at Bombay, held on July 10, 1932, a statement signed among others by Sapru was issued insisting on the conference method as an essential condition of their cooperation. The meeting also endorsed the Sapru-Jayakar resignation from the Consultative Committee.[24] The strong protests and the chance of the defection of the Liberals were among the factors which induced the Government to relent and relax. On September 5, 1932, the Viceroy indicated modification in Government attitude and announced the holding of the third RTC with a small body of Indian delegates.

On August 16, 1932, the Prime Minister's Communal Award was announced simultaneously from London and Simla. As a background to it, a Government communique stated as follows: The Minorities Committee had failed to solve the communal problem at the second RTC. The Premier had offered to give an award himself, but this was not unanimously acceptable to the members. In the final plenary session therefore he declared that, in view of the RTC members continued failure to bring about a communal settlement, the Government might have to frame and provide one. This was the rationale for the Award according to the communique.[25]

Sapru had been insisting that left to themselves the communities would sort out their differences. Gandhiji also shared the same view. Later events proved that it might have just been a pious wish. But at any rate, at the two sessions of the RTC, there was no breakthrough in the communal tangle. The British Government took obvious advantage of this. Anxious as it was to retain its hold on India even while granting it some tardy measures of reform, it reaped fun benefit of the intercommunity differences largely fanned by the rulers themselves.

The substance of the Communal Award was to fractionalize the entire electorate by giving separate recognition to a number of minorities including the Depressed Classes and assigning separate electorates to them. It was a clever way of demonstrating that Indian unity was a myth. It was indeed a great blow to the conception of Indian nationhood which had grown up and had been nurtured through a common struggle and common suffering for about a century past. But if the British wanted to break this national unity or prove that it was non-existent, some sections of the people themselves played no less a part in strengthening the hands of the rulers by placing their sectional interests above those of the common motherland.

Gandhiji who had earlier declared that he would resist the grant of separate electorates to the Depressed Classes even with his life, announced his determination to fast until the Award was modified so far as it concerned the Depressed Classes. The historic fast commenced in the Yervada jail on September 20, 1932, creating a heart breaking situation. An entire nation was in agony. A most precious life was at stake.

There was a flurry of hectic activity among the top leadership. Their anxious concern was to devise some solution so that Gandhiji's life could be saved. Madan Mohan Malaviya appealed to both the Hindu and the Depressed Class leaders to bury their differences and come to a settlement which would be acceptable to Gandhiji. Sapru and Jayakar, the two trouble shooters, immediately bestirred themselves and carried on behind the scene conciliatory moves. The Hindu leaders met in Bombay under Malaviya's presidentship. The Depressed Classes leaders headed by Ambedkar were consulted. A deputation with Sapru among others met Gandhiji more than once to discuss a new scheme based on joint electorates with adequate safeguards for the Depressed Classes. For a time the Yervada prison became a venue of hurried conferences and consultations. Sapru, Jayakar, Birla, Rajendra Prasad and Rajagopalachari explained the new scheme to Gandhiji. There was a prolonged conference in the jail among the Hindu and Depressed Classes leaders with Sapru playing a key role.[26]

A dispute arose. Dr. Ambedkar insisted that after a fixed period a referendum should decide the question of the continuation of the reservation of seats, while the Hindu leaders wanted that the reservation should automatically cease after a fixed period. Then there was a dispute over what that fixed period should be. On the fifth day of the conference, Sapru told the press: "As we could not agree on one point we wanted to consult Mahatma Gandhi. We placed the point of dispute before him and he gave his opinion on the matter. We are going back to resume our discussions and hope to see Mahatma Gandhi tomorrow morning."[27] Those were the days of feverish activity to arrive at a settlement to save Gandhiji's life. It was a race against time, for every moment was precious. Both the Caste Hindu and the Depressed Class leaders rose to their fullest stature by coming to an agreement, and Sapru drafted a cable to the Prime Minister to that effect, urging him to withdraw the separate electorates decision for the Depressed Classes. The British Government having accepted the Poona Agreement on September 26, Gandhiji broke his fast to the great relief of his countrymen. An agony ended.

Many critics have found fault with the agreement on the ground that it offers a far bigger electorate to the Depressed Classes than even an alien Prime Minister had given them. This had to be so, obviously to satisfy the demands of Ambedkar and his followers. Since Gandhiji had decided to fight for the cause of that submerged section of the society, he apparently had no objection to the weightage being given and agreed to the terms of the agreement.

Frustrated in its efforts to bypass the conference method, the Government at last yielded, though reluctantly to the insistent demand mainly from the Liberals for holding a third session of the Round Table Conference. Therefore even as the storm raised by the Communal Award and Gandhiji's fast was still blowing, preparations got off to a start to convene the RTC session.

A highly truncated RTC and much denuded of its importance and implication, was inaugurated in London by the Prime Minister on November 17, 1932, professedly to supplement the work of the two previous RTCs and to fill up important gaps. The Conference straightway buried itself with the reports of the various Committees and discussed such topics as the method of election, size of the Federal Legislature, relation between the Federal Centre and the

Units, financial matters, special powers and responsibilities of the Governor-General and the Governors and so on.

Differences cropped up on several topics and remained unresolved, while on several others, a general agreement was reached. The Financial Safeguards Committee of which Sapru was a member decided among other things, that no doubt should be left about India's capacity to maintain stability at home and credit abroad and that the Governor-General should exercise his special financial responsibilities only when he is satisfied that not to do so would endanger the Federal financial poise. Sapru was also a member of the Commercial Safeguards Committee which emphasised the avoidance of discrimination in commercial matters and urged that the partnership between India and the U.K. should remain unaltered.

Sapru was very much in favour of one Supreme Court with a Federal Division and a Division for hearing appeals from the High Courts. This would fittingly emphasize the integral character of the Federation and indeed of the country as a whole. Sapru's passion for the independence of the Judiciary found a pointed expression when he said that the constitution should provide for the appointment of judges by the Crown and guarantee of their salaries and that no religious or racial consideration should influence the appointment of judges who might be appointed from any community, Indian or European.[28]

Sapru opened the general discussion on December 23. May be, he himself had become somewhat pessimistic. This was evidence from his remark that the picture would not be complete until the White Paper was published. It was possibly the obvious loss of interest on the part of the Princes which drew out from him the remark that they must come out with a definite statement as to the size of the Federal Legislature and the allocation of seats *inter se* in view of the apparent differences on the topic. It seems he was losing patience with the Princes on account of their dilly dallying; for, he urged that the Federation must start within 12 months of the passage of the Act, keeping the door open for the Princes to come in later, in case they had not decided to join till then. In other words, he would neither let the Princes veto the Federation nor would have mere Provincial Autonomy with an unaltered Centre. He appealed to Hoare to realize that the constitution should be such as to be acceptable to the Indian people and must therefore be framed accordingly; for, he said, "... I have never known in my 30 years experience as a public man, so much of bitterness, so much of hostile feeling in Indian homes, as I have witnessed during the last few months".[29] To Gandhiji, he paid a very high tribute saying that "as far as Mr. Gandhi is concerned he sums up in his personality the highest degree of self-respect in India and the highest degree of patriotism in the country."[30]

In his reply to the discussion at the final session of the Conference, Secretary of State Samuel Hoare used soft words and sugared phrases and appeared to be anxious to meet the Indian national viewpoint. Actually what he said was a reiteration of the familiar policy of the Government without any advance towards what the Indians had been demanding. He liberally complimented Sapru saying that he was the first member of the Conference, "who fully realized the implications of this great ideal (federation) and who in those early days was much more conversant with the details of the Federation than I think any other member of the Conference".[31] While commending Sapru and his brain child, the Federation idea, he completely turned down the latter's strong plea for announcing a date for the inauguration of the Federal scheme saying that, while he did not want to see Federation drift into a mere idea, he was also not in a position to fix a firm date because of certain difficulties and complications involved in the matter.

Thus ended the story of the third RTC, mainly in words and assurances which were hardly intended to be fulfilled. Sapru along with his unfailing political collaborator, Jayakar, however did an important thing—the two together submitted on December 27, 1932, a joint memorandum for being included in the proceedings of the Conference putting forward their ideas once again in the clearest possible terms. This memorandum gives a broad outline of the Dominion constitution with a Federal Centre responsible to the Legislature. It recommends the speedy establishment of a responsible Centre, mere Provincial Autonomy being unacceptable, the inauguration of the Federation in or about the year 1935, early Indianization of the Army, precise definition of the Governor-

General's or the Governors' special powers so as not to override those of the Ministers, reduction in ordinance making to the minimum, absence of ordinance making power for the Governors, declaration of fundamental rights and so on. It would appear that through these provisions, Sapru, who did not object to the Governor-General or the Governors having special powers and responsibilities during the transition period, wanted the use of these powers to be restricted to the minimum, so that the popularly elected wing of the Government could have the fullest possible play. He wanted progress to be made in respect of Federation, because he felt that once this happened other things would gradually fall in line and get straightened. Sapru even suggested a declaration of fundamental rights to be embodied in the constitution. He did not hesitate to revert to that subject, even though earlier in the Conference itself the idea had been turned down, apparently because it sounded too radical.

Early in January 1933 Sapru and Jayakar made a joint statement summarizing the RTC results and reiterating the points made by them in their joint memorandum. They felt that despite differences there was a good deal of mutual understanding at the Conference and said that even in the face of strong resistance from certain reactionary circles in England, success could be achieved "if our countrymen organise the full force of public opinion upon a constructive plan of a satisfactory and workable Constitution".[32]

On the basis of the RTC discussions the Government framed its constitutional proposals which were published in the form of a White Paper on March 17, 1933. It came as a most disappointing document. Doubtless it did provide for a Federal Centre. But the prospects of the much desired Federation were virtually negatived by the provision that it could start only when a certain number of the States had signified their willingness to join it. In the light of this provision the solemn official assurance that mere Provincial Autonomy was not intended, sounded hollow. The Governor-General was armed with a formidable array of special powers and responsibilities, among other things, regarding Defence and External Affairs, contrary to Sapru's plea that Indian Ministers should be allowed to share power over these portfolios, at least to a limited extent. From the Provinces where it signally failed, the much condemned Dyarchy was shifted to the Centre with strong safeguards and with the vital departments placed in the Reserved hands. The Provinces were given a semblance of autonomy with a Council of Ministers working under a highly powerful Governor. Even Keith, a none too sympathetic historian of the Indian constitution, admitted that the White Paper document was heavily weighted in favour of the Conservative opinion.[33]

The White Paper had a very adverse reception from almost all sections of the public opinion in India, including the Liberals. Their dream of Dominion Status lay shattered. Their grand design of Federation stood relegated to a remote background. Even if the Federation idea were to come true at a distant date, it would be a poor Federation indeed filtered by all the safeguards that constitutional ingenuity could device. Among other things, the truly elected element in the Federal Legislature would be hopelessly criss-crossed by communal electorates making it impossible for a compact, unified and strong opposition to emerge. Together with this, the proposed Government control over the Army, External Affairs, Finance and the Services made the White Paper a dismal projection. One remembers in this connection Chintamani's pathetic lament: "The White Paper scheme was a cruel denial of the most cherished aspirations of the people of this country".[34]

Sapru too reacted sharply calling it a disappointing document. "The most outstanding features of the constitution is that far more emphasis is laid on safeguards and reservations than on Central responsibility and the possibility of its growth and expansion".[35] He wrote to Miss Harrison that the chapter on the Services was most disappointing in that, a responsible government run by public servants answerable to the Secretary of State was unthinkable.[36] Regarding this, the delegates were not allowed to discuss nine out of the ten provisions. As regards Finance, Defence and special powers of the Governor-General, none except one of the recommendations in his joint memorandum was accepted. However unlike the other Liberals he was not ready to reject the White Paper. On the contrary he emphasized the need of "material alterations and amendments".[37]

Sapru's personal disappointment can be easily imagined. All that he had been pleading for, at the RTC and from other platforms, indeed the dream of his constitutional projections, stood completely negatived. What was being proposed in the constitutional scheme was a backsliding to the Simon Commission. Yet Sapru was not exactly the person to give in. He knew that the path of constitutional advance was not smooth and that the struggle for progress in that direction must be a long, patient and sustained one, undeterred by failures and disappointments. He started looking forward to an opportunity for "material alterations and amendments" to the White Paper proposals, and the opportunity came when he was nominated to appear before the Joint Select Committee (JSC) of Parliament.

Sapru was thus one of the British Indian delegates chosen to participate in the examination of witness and discussions at the Joint Select Committee meetings. The Committee, presided over by Lord Linlithgow, was a Conservative oriented one. The Indian delegates did by no means have the status of members; they were nominated just to represent the Indian point of view before the Committee.

Having played so active a part in all the three RTCs, Sapru was most fitted to represent India's case before the Committee. Among other things he made a powerful speech on the chapter on the Services as he was not accustomed to mincing matters. No wonder that his speech was strongly resented in the Tory and the official circles. Moreover he found the political climate very unfavourable. Even such a miserly document as the White Paper was being opposed by the Tory circles under the leadership of Churchill; it was being described as a dangerous document. A tremendous campaign was also being carried on against the Indian delegates. At one stage Sapru's differences with the JSC became so acute that he thought of resigning. But he did not do so, apparently because that would amount to giving up the long and patient battle for constitutional advance.

In a personal memorandum submitted to the JSC, Sapru powerfully argued that "no constitution which fails to satisfy certain essentials will meet the needs of the situation or rally round it a sufficient body of men willing to work it in the spirit in which it should be worked."[38] He made some very important points in modification of certain aspects of the White Paper and also otherwise. First, responsibility at the Centre should be established soon enough without prolonging the transitional provisions in para 202 of the White Paper. The particular paragraph provides for certain "transitory provisions" which in the event of the Provincial part of the constitution being introduced before the constitution as a whole could empower the Governor-General to make some "temporary modifications" in the provisions of the Constitution Act pertaining to the existing Indian Legislature, the number of the Councillors and the suspension of the provisions regarding the Council of Ministers.[39] Secondly, the Army, External Affairs and Ecclesiastical Affairs, Sapru contended, should be under the Governor-General for a short transitional period. Evidently he was anxious that the complete transfer of responsibility must not be delayed in the name of a prolonged transition. Thirdly, a definite policy should be adopted regarding the Reserved departments with a view to facilitating their early transfer to Indian hands. Then again India's constitutional position within the Commonwealth, he insisted, should be definitely declared in the statute itself.

Another important point made by him was that Provisional Autonomy could be acceptable only under a Federal centre. The soundness of the point is obvious. Constitutionally, Provincial Autonomy without Central responsibility would lead to Centre Province clashes. Politically, such an autonomy will, by itself, have "the certain effects of weakening the Centre", Sapru argued.[40]

Though in favour of adult franchise, Sapru however saw the point in the Lothian Committee's arguments regarding the practical difficulties and suggested a via media, namely, to empower the Legislature to extend franchise in the light of the experience gained, so that during a period from 20 to 25 years the country could work up to the adult franchise system. The declaration of fundamental rights suggested by the Nehru Committee had been turned down by the Government. Paragraph 75 of the introduction to the White Paper recommended a royal proclamation declaring certain fundamental rights instead of embodying them statutorily. Quoting precedent from several constitutions, Sapru suggested that some of those rights could be statutorily incorporated and some others declared through a Royal proclamation. Sapru's sympathy was for a statutory embodiment of fundamental rights as would be evident from the Nehru constitution and his and Javakar's joint memorandum to the third RTC.

Sapru's main emphasis was on the transfer of responsibility to the Indian hands within the shortest possible time and with particular reference to Defence, External Affairs and Commercial Treaties. He would have some Indian say even in these matters, even though they might be reserved subjects and that too, during the transitional period. Lastly he insisted on a statutory recognition of "India's equality of status with the other Dominions as soon as she is able to set up under an Act of Parliament, a completely responsible government."[41]

Meanwhile a situation of grave anxiety was created once again by Gandhiji's 21 day fast beginning on May 8, 1933, which however was solely connected with the Harijan movement. Sapru and Jayakar, along with a few others, realised the seriousness of the situation and appealed to Gandhiji to reconsider his decision. On being released Gandhiji temporarily called off the civil disobedience movement and urged the Government to set free the political prisoners. The Government however refused to oblige. Sapru and Jayakar took up the cause and wrote to Hoare requesting him to release the political prisoners in view of Gandhiji's decision regarding the suspension of the civil disobedience movement.[42] Hoare however was not satisfied with temporary suspension and would not relent. The Government of India Act 1935 came in for severe criticism from almost all sections of Indian opinion. What to speak of the Congress, even the Liberals who were never extravagant in their demands, strongly disapproved of it. Jinnah, the undisputed leader of the Muslims, was highly critical of it. The Act was a child of compromise—the British Government was seeking to reconcile the view points of the Labour and the Tories at home and the communalists and nationalists in India. In doing so, they put the maximum premium upon the conservative and communal view point and let the nationalist demands go almost by default. Under it, all others might have gained in varying degrees, but India's national aspirations lost grievously.

By giving the Princes the option to join or not to join the Federation, the Act conceded them a virtual, though indirect, veto and managed to put the grand design into cold storage. By refusing to promise or assure Dominion Status in a new Preamble to the Act and retaining the Preamble to the Act of 1919, the new constitution only betrayed its author's ominous mental reservations. Indeed the Centre minus Federation with enormous discretionary powers put in the Governor-General's hands was old wine in a new bottle, a reenactment of the 1919 Act in many respects. The discredited Dyarchy was transferred from the Provinces to a seat of honour at the Centre. Under an all powerful Governor-General, responsibility at the Centre became a farce. The Provinces were invested with a political personality, at least technically. But the Provincial Governors were there with an equally formidable set of extraordinary powers to undermine the theoretically given autonomy. No wonder that Keith describes the new constitution as a "legislative monostrosity".

It may be recalled that apart from Federation and Dominion Status, Sapru pleaded strongly for the association of the Indians with the administration of Defence and External Affairs. But the Act reserved both these vital portfolios entirely in the authority of the Governor-General. The Act was born in mistrust, hedged in with enormous caution and ominous safeguards.

It was the Liberals who had cooperated with the Government at almost every stage of the constitution making and still entertained some hope about it. They themselves felt completely let down. They were bitter and some of them uncompromisingly bitter.

Sapru was strongly critical but was not in favour of rejection. To do so would, in his opinion, be a philosophy of negation. His criticism though trenchant was constructive. He would always try to find out a via media between two conflicting viewpoints and never give up his quest for a reasonable solution. He would not like the constitution making process to come to a dead halt. In this respect he was strikingly different from some of his Liberal colleagues. Indeed he had been having differences with the Liberal Party for some time past and had virtually severed connection with the party since the first RTC. Replying to S.M. Basu's invitation to attend the National Liberal Federation meeting in September 1932, Sapru wrote to him declining the invitation, saying that for nearly two years he had been out of the Federation. The difference of opinion obviously centred, among other things, round the Communal Award which unlike the Liberals, he was not ready to reject. He wrote: "I realise that separate electorates are bad, that joint electorates are good, but unfortunately I also realize that you cannot have joint electorates without mutual understanding ..."[43] Chintamani took a more and more extreme line and had differences with Sapru despite their close friendship. But in or outside the Party, Sapru continued to represent the finest spirit of liberalism like Gandhiji remaining theoretically outside the Congress Party at a later stage.

REFERENCES

1. Dutt, Iswara, *The Street of Ink, op. cit.*, p. viii.
2. Tara Chand, *History of the Freedom Movement in India*, Vol. IV (New Delhi: Publications Division, Ministry of Information and Broadcasting, Government of India), 1967.
3. *Proceedings of the First Round Table Conference.*
4. *Ibid.*
5. *Ibid.*
6. Panikar, K.M., *His Highness the Maharaja of Bikaner* (Bombay: Asia), 1955.
7. Setalvad, *Recollections and Reflections, op. cit.*
8. *Ibid.*
9. *Proceedings of the First Round Table Conference.*
10. *Indian Annual Register*, Vol. I, 1931.
11. *Proceedings of the First Round Table Conference.*
12. *Indian Annual Register*, Vol. I, 1931.
13. *Sapru Papers,* J 68, February 27, 1931.
14. *Ibid.*, J 69, February 28, 1931.
15. *Jayakar Papers*, File No. 454, Letter 80, May 8, 1931 (New Delhi: National Archives).
16. *Ibid.*, Letter 101, May 30, 1931.
17. *Ibid.*
18. Tara Chand, *History of the Freedom Movement in India*, Vol. IV, *op. cit.*
19. *Report of the Federal Structure and Minorities Committees Proceedings of the RTC, Second Session.*
20. *Report of the RTC. Second Session.*
21. *Ibid.*

22. *Ibid.*
23. *Indian Annual Register*, Vol. II, 1932.
24. *Ibid.*
25. *Ibid.*
26. *Ibid.*
27. *Ibid.*
28. *Ibid.*
29. *Ibid.*
30. *Ibid.*
31. *Ibid.*
32. *Ibid.*, Vol. I., 1933.
33. Keith, A.B., *A Constitutional History of India* (London: Methuen), 1937.
34. Chintamani. C.Y., *Indian Politics Since Mutiny, op. cit.*
35. *Indian Annual Register*, Vol. I, 1933.
36. *Sapru Papers*, H 194, March 19, 1933.
37. *Indian Annual Register*, Vol. I, 1933.
38. *Parliamentary Papers, House of Commons*, Vol. III.
39. *White Papers*, para 202.
40. *Parliamentary Papers, House of Commons*, Vol. III.
41. *Ibid.*
42. *Sapru Papers*, H 229, May 10, 1933.
43. *Ibid.*, B 96, September 5, 1932.

4

ON THE LEGAL HORIZON

In those twilight days of early Colonial rule, the scope of employment for the rising intelligentsia was all too meagre. Government service was of course the most tempting prospect, but that was bound to be limited. Necessarily, Law became one of the easily available avenues to the educated youth. But Law was not just a means for earning livelihood. To those who wanted to shine as judges or lawyers or otherwise distinguish themselves in society, it offered an ample opportunity. It is not of little significance that in those days the topmost men of the country's public life were drawn from the profession of law. It was one profession which, apart from everything else, afforded a rare opportunity of entry to the field of politics and public life.

To opt for Law was thus an easy and almost a natural choice for Sapru. He started practice in Moradabad in 1896 at a young age but had to pass through an idle period inevitable in almost all legal career. However, he did not waste any opportunity that came his way. By hard and diligent study he started building the foundation of his astonishing legal erudition of the later days. Very soon he realized that the District Bar of Moradabad was too small and too stagnant for his gradually unfolding spirit. Generally the position of the District Bar was by no means insignificant. It produced many men of eminence. Many of its members occupied important positions in different spheres of public life. Nevertheless it could not obviously offer the same scope and opportunity as the High Court Bar. Sapru's mind was reaching out for higher attainments—his spirit was not to be confined within the narrow limits of the district courts. Sapru therefore decided to shift to the Allahabad High Court, and this he did in 1898, thus crossing the first watershed of his life.

The story of Sapru's arrival at Allahabad has been told by Dr. Sachchidananda Sinha, one of his closest friends and his senior at the Allahabad High Court Bar by two years.[1] It is also the story of a life long friendship that never flagged. Dr. Sinha had joined the Allahabad High Court Bar in 1896. Two years later Satya Charan Mukherji, a well known advocate, came to him one day with a request. He told Dr. Sinha that he had met "a fine type of a brilliant Kashmiri youth" at Moradabad who was ambitious enough to think of coming to the Allahabad High Court to make his fortune. But since Mukherji himself would be otherwise busy on the day of his arrival, he requested Dr. Sinha to receive the young man at the railway station. On the appointed day Dr. Sinha went to the station, and could spot Sapru coming out of a second class carriage looking 'spick and span'. It was love at first sight, and the friendship between the two became deep and abiding. Dr. Sinha took him to his 7 Elgin Road house. Sapru called him 'Bhai Saheb' and asked Sinha to call him by his pet name 'Makhanji'. Incidentally Sinha's 7 Elgin Road house also became a haunt of the elite even as Sapru's own 19 Albert Road residence became, in a far greater measure at a later date. Dr. Sinha stayed at Allahabad till 1910 when, with his election to the Imperial Legislative Council, he shifted to Calcutta. He later became the first President of the Indian Constituent Assembly.

Sapru's initial years at the Allahabad High Court were naturally comparatively briefless ones. But as at Moradabad, here also he did not just vegetate or idle away his time. Determined as he was to rise in his profession, he devoted himself to a study of the fundamental principles of Law as well as its different branches. By a dedicated sense of study and perseverance and with his natural intellectual brilliance, he built up the edifice of his remarkable legal erudition of which the foundation had been laid at Moradabad. He established academic reputation by taking the Master of Laws degree in 1900 and by becoming a Doctor of Laws in 1902. He thus became Dr. Tej Bahadur Sapru. In 1903 he took up part-time Law Lecturership, at Allahabad Muir Central College. Legal education had till then not been put on a sound footing and there was a good deal of laxity in it. The Allahabad University having been a mere examining body, Law used to be taught at the Muir Central College which had a staff of a Law Professor and some part-time Lecturers. However Sapru took up his task in right earnest as was only characteristic of him. Among his pupils were some eminent lawyers of U.P. like Dr. K.N. Katju. In 1906 Sapru was enrolled as an advocate. This was a great distinction for the young lawyer, since it put him on par with the British members of the Bar. The hard labour he did during the previous years started fetching him rich dividends. He came to be known as one of the most learned lawyers having mastery over almost all branches of Law and jurisprudence.

The history of the Allahabad High Court is briefly this. It was the fourth oldest High Court in India. The British acquired certain areas which from 1835 came to be known as the North-Western Provinces. Following the annexation of Oudh in 1856, a Judicial Commissioner's court was set up there. But by Royal Letters Patent of March 17, 1866, a separate High Court was set up for the North-Western Provinces at Agra replacing the Sudder Diwanni Adalat. Sir Walter Morgan became the first Chief Justice of the Court. Oudh, however, continued to have its own judicial arrangement as before. In 1902 the North-Western Provinces was reconstituted to form the United Provinces of Agra and Oudh, the latter still remaining separate judicially. Oudh however came to have a Chief Court replacing the Judicial Commissioner's Court in 1925. The North-Western Provinces High Court sat at Agra from 1866 to 1868 and thereafter shifted to Allahabad where it has been functioning since then. The Oudh Chief Court was amalgamated with the Allahabad High Court by the U.P. Amalgamation of High Court Order of 1948. Lucknow now has a Bench of the High Court.

The Allahabad High Court whose centenary was celebrated in 1966 has had a remarkable tradition. The first Indian judge of the High Court was Mr. Justice Mahmood, second son of the celebrated Sir Syed Ahmad Khan, and himself a man of profound learning. Sapru came in close touch with him and was deeply impressed by his powerful personality as well as his high legal erudition. Sapru paid him a rich tribute by referring among other qualities of Mahmood, to "his deep and varied learning", "his independence" and "his strong sympathies with the poor and the oppressed."[2] Those, were the shining days of the Indian Judiciary when there was a galaxy of brilliant Indian judges like Justice Mahmood at Allahabad and Sir Gurudam Banerji, Muthu Swami Aiyer and others elsewhere in the country. Another distinguished Indian judge of the Allahabad High Court was Pramoda Charan Banerji to whose eminence Sapru himself testifies.[3] A number of other outstanding European and Indian Judges sat on the Bench of the Court whose individual, suffice it to say, that the Allahabad High Court produced some very eminent judges, just as the High Court Bar produced some distinguished advocates, jurists opinion.

Sapru himself describes the condition of the High Court Bar when he joined it thus: "In 1898 when I shifted to the High Court and unlearned junior, the towering personalities in the profession were Mr. Conlan, Mr. (afterwards Sir) Walter Colvin, Mr. Dwarkanath Banerji, among the representatives of the English Bar, Pandit (afterwards Sir) Sunderlal, Mr. Chaudhry (Jogendra Nath) and Pandit Moti Lal Nehru ... To us Juniors of those days they were awe inspiring names and some of us felt they were unapproachable."[4] At that time the Bar was mostly dominated by the Europeans among whom there were some brilliant advocates. But the Indian lawyers had also come up to claim equal distinction in forensic skill. Sunderlal, Jogendra Nath and Munshi Ram Prasad were the most outstanding among them. Sapru himself was associated with Jogendra Nath in several cases. Moti Lal Nehru had also come up to the forefront by the sharpness of his intellect and his engaging advocacy; he was the "rising star" among the leaders of the Bar.[5] Another luminary rising on the legal firmament was Pandit Madan Mohan Malaviya for whom Sapru had a high regard. Later he gave up his legal practice to serve the cause of the country, as did Motilal. It is interesting to note that despite political differences, Sapru continued to have a high regard for Madan Mohan and his leadership. If it was an era of great judges, it was also an era of great advocates.

However it was not at all smooth sailing for the Indian members of the Bar when Sapru joined it. Indeed they had initially to suffer from various disabilities compared to their European colleagues, even though they were in no way inferior to the latter. There were two types of advocates practising at that time—the barristers of the English and the Irish Bars and the Scottish advocates on the one hand, and the Indian vakils enrolled by the High Court on the other. Most of the practising Barristers having been Europeans, used to look down upon the "native vakils".[6] The two categories had their respective associations too. Pandit Ayodhyanath was the first president of the Vakils' Association. There was a third category of lawyers—the Indian Barristers who were not always acceptable to the first category and hence formed their own separate association. Incidentally all the three associations merged together to form the Allahabad High Court Bar Association in 1957.

Thus the Indian vakils had to start their career with an initial disadvantage, that is, with a mark of racial inferiority unjustly branded on them. But gradually the rules changed and the vakils who could get the LL.D. degree of the Allahabad University could be enrolled. The Chief Justice was empowered to elevate a vakil to the status of an advocate, provided he was a man of outstanding merit. The first batch of vakils who were made advocates in 1896 included Sunderlal, Munshi Ram Prasad, Jogendra Nath and Motilal Nehru. Sapru himself was one of the outstanding vakils raised to the status of an advocate. Despite there being some brilliant European advocates, the leadership of the Bar actually belonged to such Indian lawyers as mentioned above.

The Allahabad Bar has always been reputed as one of the strongest in the country. In those days not only many of its members distinguished themselves as advocates and jurists but personalities like Motilal Nehru, Madan Mohan Malaviya and others also came to occupy the front rank among the leadership of the country. India's first Prime Minister and the maker of modern India joined the Allahabad Bar in 1912, although his association with it was all too brief. Sapru belonged to that galaxy of great advocates who not only shed lustre upon their profession but also played a vital role in the public life of the country. Although Law is a jealous mistress, Sapru nevertheless found time to remain a dynamic politician almost till the end of his life. Dr. K.N. Katju who attended Supru's chamber from 1914 onwards says: "Not only numerous beginners have sat at his feet but his chamber has been the nursery of judges. He is the soul of honour and his uprightness of conduct and his professional rectitude have been a beaconlight to lawyers throughout the United Provinces."[7] The two most promising lawyers of those days in the Allahabad High Court were Dr. Satish Chandra Banerji and Dr. Sapru, both being equally erudite. The former died prematurely in 1915, while the latter equipped with his early study and natural brilliance, made a spectacular rise in the profession. Sapru was steeped in the British system of jurisprudence and came to have a high admiration for it. He specialized in civil and constitutional law and became a constitution maker at later date. Indeed few could equal him in the knowledge of constitutional law. This greatly coloured his political philosophy which, in brief, was the philosophy of constitutionalism.

As already noted, Sapru utilized his waiting period, though comparatively short, for a wide ranging study and perseverance. The result was that it was not long before he earned reputation as a very learned lawyer. He held briefs for several eminent seniors like Motilal and Madan Mohan, and had by 1905 built up a good junior practice, so much so that he had to give up his Law Lecturership at the Muir Central College to be able to devote more time to his profession. By 1906 he found himself in an established position at the Bar. His practice was mostly on the civil side, though he was equally good in criminal matters as well.

The way he shot into prominence is interesting to recall. After about ten years practice he got a very significant opportunity to show his talents. Pitted against some celebrities of the Bar, he argued a Hindu Law case so impressively that the Bench (including the then Chief Justice Sir Henry Richards) openly congratulated him. In 1912, he opposed a lawyer of the standing of Sir Rashbehari Ghosh at the Oudh Chief Court where he was engaged in some commercial cases and also in a Waqf case at the High Court in 1916. In this way he earned reputation as a very brilliant advocate and built up a lucrative practice. He was very much in demand not only in his home province but all over the country. Litigants from different walks of life, including the native princes flocked to him with their briefs. Regarding his style of advocacy, Mr. Justice Nasirullah Beg, a former Chief Justice of the Allahabad High Court, observed that his flow of erudition and array of arguments "reminded one of the incessant waves of an ocean".[8]

Sapru rose to great heights, apart from his legal learning, by virtue of the sheer moral tone of his character and his professional rectitude. He set up standards of behaviour not easily to be matched. He never believed in backdoor methods of success. His half a century long association with Law was a spotless record of professional integrity of the highest order.

One more important point was his firm faith in the British system of justice and in the process of constitutional progress. It was his training at the hard school of Law that made him almost a rigid constitutionalist and he could always bring a very rational and dispassionate mind to bear upon political questions. It was largely in the courts of law that the politician Sapru was made.

By the beginning of 1920, Dr. Tej Bahadur Sapru was recognised as a lawyer of national standing, whose services were widely sought across British India as well as in different Indian States.[9] In fact, before the end of the first quarter of 1920, Sapru had turned down a High Court Judgeship (letter of 7 April, written by Liakat Ali from Bhopal [SP I, No. A.41]). Over the years, Sapru would receive and turn down similar offers, though he would never talk about it openly. Professor Rushbrook Williams, an admirer and friend observed years afterwards: "Sapru was one of these very, very, learned lawyers and he was sought all over India for the profoundity of his views...Most of his work was done in Chambers and he used to refer to himself with a twinkle in his eye as a 'native pleader'. And his legal eminence, of course, carried him to membership of the Privy Council and to be an Honorary Bench of Lincoln's Inn ... He was a great man."[10]

Towards the end of 1920, Sapru was appointed Law Member in the Viceroy's Executive Council, a post that he took formal charge of on 20th December, 1920. In the wake of the sweeping changes the political scene was undergoing as a result of "the emergence of the charismatic leadership of Gandhiji and the non-cooperation movement initiated by him ... Sapru was well aware that the

Government was depending on Moderate support and also that in joining the Viceroy's Executive Council as Law Member he was taking upon himself a very uneasy responsibility", comments Bose.[11]

Sapru's spell as Law Member coincided with a momentous period in Indian history. The story of those years, particularly the first non-cooperation movement launched by the Congress and the large scale arrests that accompanied it is well known.[12] Along with that came reactionary backlash in the shape of the diehardism of the Provincial Governors and various British Members of Parliament, an example of which was the infamous 'steel frame' speech of Lloyd George. "He followed Sir Sankara Nair, who had resigned after the Punjab disturbances", noted C.F. Andrews. "No more difficult post could have been offered to anyone at such a critical time and it required resolution on his part to accept it. I know from personal experience how greatly the Viceroy relied on his counsel, and how frank Dr. Sapru was in offering unpalatable advice"[13]

Even as the visit of the Prince of Wales, scheduled for the winter of 1921 drew near, the non-cooperation movement showed no sign of subsiding. Arrests were commonplace now and Sapru, who had long been urging the Viceroy to seek further liberalization of the constitutional arrangements under the 1919 Act, emphasised that even the Liberals and constitutionalists who had not been in favour of non-cooperation, would not blindly support the Government in the wide scale arrests, prosecutions, and coercive action against the non-cooperators. The situation was further complicated by the prosecution of certain Khilafat leaders, even as the Viceroy considered possible solutions to the impasse.[14]

It was at this stage that the possibility of a round table conference was mooted by Sapru. By now, the Congress was about to meet at Ahmedabad for its annual session scheduled for December 1921.

Soon afterwards, the Congress met at Ahmedabad in the last week of December for the annual session and rejected Lord Reading's offer of a round table conference, and gave Mahatma Gandhi a *carte blanc* for the inauguration of civil disobedience in Bardoli. By now the Viceroy was facing intense pressure from the

British members of his Executive Council as well as his Governors for the arrest of the Mahatma.

The Mahatma was prosecuted for sedition and sentenced to six years' prison. Soon afterwards, Sapru tendered his resignation from the position of Law Member in the Viceroy's Executive Council. In England the die-hards were becoming more vociferous; the Secretary of State, Montagu had resigned and his place was taken by Lord Peel; and the Indian members of the Council were finding themselves unable to influence Government policies in the wake of the attitude of a majority of the British Governors and other administrators.

Eventually, Sapru's resignation was accepted, effective from 8th February 1923. H.N. Kunzru, Tej Bahadur Sapru's life long friend, notes what Lord Reading told his out going Law Member: "Sapru, you have isolated me, because there is no other member of the Executive Council who is in touch with Indian public opinion."[15]

Since Sapru was Law Member during a period that is popularly remembered for the civil disobedience movement, it may be relevant to emphasise here that as Law Member Sapru undertook certain other measures which had long-term significance for India. One of these concerned the then existing racial discrimination in the sphere of the administration of law and justice. This had been left unchanged for several decades, and was handed over from the opposition of the British to the Ilbert Bill. In a move of far-reaching importance, Sapru presided over a committee set up for the purpose of ending the blatant discrimination.

Yet another important step was related to the repeal of the repressive Press Act of 1910 and the Newspapers (Incitement to Offences) Act of 1908. These Acts "introduced during the earlier stormy decade sought virtually to muzzle the press by empowering the Executive to demand security money from where ever deemed necessary ... [which] could be forfeited for publishing 'objectionable matters' at the unquestioned discretion of an all-powerful Executive. The Act was vigorously enforced during the war years punishing a very large number of persons and periodicals. A Government appointed press committee headed by Sapru recommended the repeal of these two measures."[16]

The Committee headed by Sapru further recommended that the confiscation of 'openly seditious publications' needed to become subject of judicial review, through making changes in the Sea Customs and Post Offices Acts, as well as through resorting to relevant provisions of the Indian Penal Code. As a consequence of Sapru's effort in this area, Act No. XIV of 1922, repealing the 1908 and 1910 Acts and taking cognizance of the changes recommended, was passed; receiving the Viceroy and Governor-General's assent in March 1922, a short while before Sapru resigned from the Law Membership.

Among other issues that Sapru took up while Law Member was the question of the reorganisation of the Bar in India, for which he made certain recommendations. The result was the appointment of a Committee presided over by Sir Edward Chamier, which, in turn, led to the passage of the Indian Bar Councils Act in 1926 (though this Act only partially satisfied Sapru as far as its provisions, duties and powers conferred were concerned).[17] Noted P.N. Sapru, "While Law Member of Lord Reading's Cabinet, he formed the opinion that our legal processes were far too dilatory and he wrote for the benefit of his colleagues a note on the law's delays which subsequently led to appointment of the Chief Justice Committee under the Chairmanship of Sir George Rankin, Chief Justice of Calcutta. Later, in his capacity as co-opted member of the committee he indicated in another note the changes that were needed to speed up the judicial process."[18]

The Indianization of the Army, an issue that Sapru worked for over the ensuing decades too, was keenly supported by him during his tenure as Law Member (and, consequently, a member of the Defence Committee). In this context, he took a stem stand in the Council over the 'steel frame' speech of Lloyd George, echoed by that of the Commander-in-Chief, questioning whether it would ever be possible to completely eliminate the British element from the army and civil service of India. Not just as Law Member, but in every other context too, Tej Bahadur's approach to a problem was "...not that of a mere lawyer but that of a jurist who had a wide vision of the law ... His immense legal learning made him look at even political questions from a legal point of view and that accounts for his zeal for civil liberties".[19]

After resignation from the Law Membership (effective February 8, 1923), Sapru returned to the Allahabad High Court Bar and his legal practice, from where he was to lead the Allahabad Bar until his prolonged illness in 1946.

Soon thereafter, in the spring of 1923, Sapru was asked to represent British India at the Imperial Conference to be held in London later that year. As there had been a recent policy decision taken by the British Government which was adverse to the Indians in Kenya, Sapru was urged by many, including his close associates, to boycott the conference in protest. This was not Sapru's way, however. On 4th June, 1923, Sapru telegraphed the Viceroy, accepting the appointment.[20]

1924 was also the year that Sapru wrote a critique of the constitution. This came out in its published form—*The Indian Constitution: A Note on Its Working* in 1926.[21] In his capacity as President of the National Convention, of which Annie Besant was the General Secretary, Sapru also collaborated with him as the principal architect of a "Bill to constitute within the British Empire a Commonwealth of India," better known as the Commonwealth of India Bill, that December.[22] It was in this Bill (presented to the House of Commons in 1925 by George Lansbury), that fundamental rights were placed on a juristic footing for the first time.

Over the next few years, alongside his legal work, Sapru continued to follow political developments very keenly. By now Sapru's legal eminence was recognised even outside India, though as C.F. Andrews stated in a different context, voicing the opinion of an entire generation of contemporaries, while Sapru "took up civil and criminal cases as a matter of practice and was a keen lawyer ... his heart had always been in constitutional law; and on this subject with an authority than that of any contemporary lawyer in India."[23]

Given Sapru's standing, it is scarcely surprising that in 1927 the Bar Association of Turkey honoured the famous Indian lawyer by conferring membership on him! 1927 was also the year when Sapru served as the President of the National Liberal Federation for the second time; the first having been in 1923.

At its Madras session in December 1927, the Congress Party adopted the attainment of complete independence for India as its objective, and announced that in protest against the non-inclusion of any Indian in the Simon Commission, and in response to Birkenhead's challenge, the Congress would draft a constitution for India, in association with other parties.

The all-white Simon Commission arrived in India in February 1928, to be met by protests, black-flags, and sustained boycott. This situation continued as the Commission made its 'blood-red progress', as Gandhi called it, across India. While the Commission was touring India, Indian political leaders met to discuss a future constitution. In February 1928 an All-Parties Conference met at Delhi, under the chairmanship of Dr. Ansari, the Congress President, and voted for full responsible government. Three months later, at the All-Parties Conference held in May, a committee was appointed with Motilal Nehru as its chairman, to determine the principles of the constitution for India. Sapru participated whole-heartedly as an active principal member of this Nehru Committee on constitutional reforms, between May to August.

The Nehru Committee completed its work in August. Its report visualised full responsible government for India, and recognised that a place would have to be found for the Indian States. The 'Nehru Report' further conceived of a unitary form of government for India by vesting the residuary power in the central government, rather than the provincial governments. This draft constitution also stood for adult franchise, a bicameral legislature, an independent judiciary with a Supreme Court as its apex, and a joint electorate for all the communities, with reservation of seats for Muslims in the Muslim minority provinces, but no such reservation in Muslim majority provinces. Other recommendations included the constitution of Sind as a separate province.

This Report "drafted by Motilal Nehru with the help of his son, before Tej Bahadur Sapru took a hand ... was an attempt to reconcile the conflicting claims of the various religious communities, and to find a via media between the radicalism of the Indian National Congress and the conservatism of the Indian Liberals. In the event, the Nehru Report could not solve the communal tangle, as the British

Government was an invisible third party in the possession of the cake..."[24]

In December 1928, representatives of eighty seven parties met at Calcutta in an All-Parties All India Conference to consider and approve the Nehru Report. At the Conference, Sapru in his speech, called upon Jinnah and all the other participants 'as practical statesman' to 'try and solve the problem and not be misled by arithmetical figures'. However, Jinnah demanded certain weightages for the Muslims, and went on to lead a section that had objections to the Report. Jinnah's opposition was out voted by the majority view. This was a turning point in Indian history, for Jinnah now conclusively parted company with the Congress.

The Report also came under fire from some of the younger Congress leaders, including Subhas Chandra Bose and Jawaharlal Nehru, but at the Calcutta Congress session of December 1928 mediation by Gandhi enabled a compromise acceptable to both sides within the Congress. Consequently, it "was agreed that the Congress would accept the whole of the Nehru Report, including the Dominion Status formula, but if it was not accepted by the British Government within a year, the Congress would opt for complete independence, and fight for it, if necessary, by invoking civil disobedience."[25]

REFERENCES

1. Fifty Years with Sir Tej Bahadur Sapru, *Hindusthan Review*, March, 1949.
2. Syed Mahmood as Judge, Tej Bahadur Sapru, *Hindusthan Review*, May 1903.
3. *Ibid.*
4. In Memorium, the late Jogindra Nath Choudhry, Allahabad High Court Centenary Commemoration, Vol. I.
5. *Ibid.*
6. Varma, S.N., *History of Allahabad High Court Bar Association*, Allahabad H.C. Centenary Commemoration, Vol. I.
7. Katju, K.N., *Reminiscences and Experiments in Advocacy* (Allahabad: Kitabistan), 1956.
8. Speech, Allahabad High Court Centenary Commemoration, Vol. II.
9. Raina (ed.), *Tej Bahadur Sapru—Responsa: Selected Legal Opinions, op. cit.*, pp. vii-viii.

10. Rushbrook, Williams, C.F., in Mss. Eur. R & T. 130, recorded June and August 1976, British Library Oriental and India Office Collections (OIOC).
11. Bose, *Tej Bahadur Sapru, op. cit*., pp. 44-45.
12. Pandey, B.N., *The Break-Up of British India* (London: Macmillan & Co.), 1969.
13. Williams, Rushbrook (ed.), *Great Men of India, op. cit*., pp. 398-99.
14. Nanda, B.R., *The Making of a Nation: India's Road to Independence* (New Delhi: Harper Collins India Pvt. Ltd.), 1998, p. 158.
15. Kunzru in *Commemoration Volume*, New Delhi, 1976.
16. Bose, *Tej Bahadur Sapru, op. cit.*
17. Presidential Address, *First United Province of Agra and Oudh Lawyer's Conference*, Allahabad, 6-7, November, 1938, pp. 8-9.
18. Raina (ed.), *Tej Bahadur Sapru—Responsa: Selected Legal Opinions, op. cit*., pp. xvii-xviii.
19. Raina, K.N. and V. Gopala Ratnam (eds.), *Tej Bahadur Sapru: Profiles and Tributes, op. cit*., p. 64.
20. Telegram No. 185, Mss Eur 238/25/OIOC.
21. Sapru, T.S., *The Indian Constitution: A Note on Its Working* (Madras: Adyar), 1926.
22. Bose, *Tej Bahadur Sapru, op. cit*., pp. 61-63.
23. Williams, Rushbrook (ed.), *Great Men of India, op. cit*., p. 397.
24. Nanda, B.R., *The Making of a Nation: India's Road to Independence, op. cit*., pp. 200-201.
25. *Ibid*., p. 201.

5

THE HINDU-MUSLIM RELATIONS

A number of British statesmen and publicists have made facile generalizations about the irreconcilable nature of Hindu-Muslim antagonisms and have laid undue emphasis on the barriers of race, culture, law and social custom, which, they allege, keep these two great communities apart. The extracts which we give below, show how persistent this view has been.

As far back as 1892, while introducing in the House of Commons a Bill relating to the Government of India, Mr (afterwards Lord) Curzon described the Indian people as:

"Sundered into irreconcilable camps by differences of caste, of religion, of custom, which held men fast bound during their life time and the rigour of which is not abated even beyond the grave..."[1]

Nearly forty years later, the *Indian Statutory Commission* expressed itself in similar way:

"It would be an utter misapprehension to suppose that Hindu-Muslim antagonism is analogous to the separation between religious denominations in contemporary Europe. Differences of race, a different system of law, and the absence of inter-marriage constitute a far more effective barrier. It is a basic opposition, manifesting itself at every turn in social custom and economic competition, as well as in mutually religious antipathy."[2]

According to the Joint Committee on Indian Constitutional Reform: "... the difference between the two [Hindu and Muslim] is not only one of religion in the stricter sense, but also of law and of culture. They may be said indeed to represent two distinct and separate civilizations."[3]

Sir Reginald Coupland observes: "... the main distinction [between the Hindu Muslim] is not physical but cultural. It is the outcome of two sharply contrasted religions and of the social systems, the ways of life and thought they have inspired."[4]

The historic correctness of Sir Tej Bhadur Sapru's view, in so far as it bears question of the feasibility of the two communities living together in political unity with mutual toleration and respect for each other's religion and culture, have been examined.

For over 1000 years, Muslims and Hindus in India have lived together. The first contact between them was a peaceful one. Arabs had intimate relations with India from very ancient times. They began with commerce and trade and, as these grew, trade routes by land and sea came to be established. In course of time, settlements of Muslim traders flourished in the South. These drew more Muslims to India and they brought with them their distinct pattern of culture. They had, in their native home, developed great literatures in Arabic and Persian, and these ideas and movements continued to flow to India from Arabia, Iraq, Iran and other places.[5] The Muslims were welcomed in India by Hindu potentates in keeping with the prevailing policy of religious toleration. Mosques were allowed to be built and religious propaganda permitted. Eclecticism, like toleration, had been a feature of the Hindu faith even in those times and Muslims were thus able, in course of time, to establish centres in the South, where, besides exchange of goods and commodities, an exchange of ideas also took place. The settlers did not confine their social life and intercourse to their own community. They spread amongst the people and, owing thereto, a number of communities of mixed descent came into existence, who helped in the process of approximation.

It was, however, difficult for Hinduism to assimilate these new settlers completely as it had in the past absorbed successive immigrants like the Scythians, Sakas and Huns. But, though a general fusion was impossible, the new arrivals amongst the Muslims in their turn freely mixed with the people around them and gradually spread themselves over the country. They came to acquire considerable influence in politics and society. Instances were not unknown of Muslim ministers and advisers being employed by Hindu

Kings even in those early days. An identity of interest was often established between the employer and the employed. When eventually Muslim waves of conquest invaded India, Indian Muslims fought side by side with Hindu Kings in resisting the Muslim invaders, and religious affinity gave place to other loyalties born of contract, understanding and common political allegiance.

Later, came a horde of Muslim invaders who looted the country. But, even with reference to these plundering expeditions, it can be said with truth that after the first lust of conquest had spent itself, human forces began to operate which interknit the two communities. The Muslims, unlike other invaders, made India their home and were not merely birds of passage bent upon making the best of their temporary rule. Instances were not rare of Hindu chieftains and soldiers fighting under Muslim rulers against Hindus and Muslims alike. Similarly, Muslim captains and soldiers fought by the side of Hindu Rajas. Religious toleration, the outstanding feature of Hinduism through the ages, helped the growth of these affinities, and neither political feuds nor armed skirmishes ever came in the way of its maintenance.

Making India their home, the Indian Muslims took naturally to the Indian languages. They thus became a part of the people surrounding them. There was also considerable racial penetration. Trade and industry produced new relationships. An equally potent factor in this process was the occupational division of society into professional and other classes to which Hindus and Muslims alike belonged—peasants, landlords, traders, artisans, labourers, soldiers, government servants, etc. Many Hindu sub-castes, whose main occupation was government service, formed a political link between the Muslim Rulers and their Hindu subjects. Within each class, Hindus and Muslims were often indistinguishable from each other, as they are now, in dress, housing, etiquette or manners, whether in villages or in towns. They joined in each others festivals. The position of women, the age of marriage and even some wedding and other rituals were uniform within a class and common to its Hindu and Muslim members. A particular class held together by many considerations and interests which cut across religious cleavage.

The ethical standards set up by Hindus and Muslims were essentially similar.

Subsequently, with the advent of the Mughals, this process became more marked. The achievements of Emperors like Sher-Shah and Akbar in terms of toleration are too well known to be repeated here. The imperial court extended its patronage to Hindu as well as Muslim scholars and became their meeting ground. Hindus studied Arabic and Persian, and some of their Persian writings have endured to the present day. As early as the eleventh century, Alberuni, a great Muslim scholar, had set the example by mastering the intricacies of Sanskrit and his account and appreciation of Hindu achievements in science and philosophy are of permanent value. In the sixteenth and seventeenth centuries, Muslim scholars translated important Sanskrit works into Persian. Two illustrious promoters of such a rapprochement are Amir Khusrau and Prince Dara Shikoh. Khusrau was the most famous poet of his time, as also the most brilliant man of letters at the court of the Delhi Emperor. A prolific writer, he enjoys popularity even to the present day. He could write and speak Hindi well. His contribution to Indian music will be noticed below. Prince Dara Shikoh was an accomplished scholar and a great admirer of Hindu philosophy and Sanskrit learning. Under his auspices a Persian translation of the *Upanishads* was made, as also of the *Bhagavat Gita* and *Yoga Vasistha*. He wrote a number of learned works and collected around himself a notable band of scholars, with the intention of building a bridge between Hindu and Muslim cultures. Such examples can be multiplied almost indefinitely. In fact, the greater part of the literary activity of India between the fourteenth and nineteenth centuries, represents Hindu-Muslim collaboration in providing a distinctly Indian literature, which constituted one of the most significant developments indicating the interaction of reciprocal influences.

Even after the break-up of the Mughal Empire owing to the revolt of the outlying Sultanates and the increasing might of the Marathas, the edifice of Hindu-Muslim cooperation, built up by centuries of previous integration, was maintained with as little damage as possible. The lesson of the past was not forgotten that such cooperation had eased administration and stood the severest test of adverse circumstances. In the new states, which rose from the ruins of the Mughal Empire, the privileges and positions previously given to Hindus were maintained, and Rajputs, Marathas, Sikhs and Jats enjoyed, as before, important offices and the vital power of political direction. The momentum given to unifying forces by the Mughal Empire, as stated above, was maintained and the traditions of common administrative practices continued as before till the Marathas engulfed the Muslim Empire and captured the very seat of power at Delhi.

This is the true record of the past, strange and unbelievable as it may seem in the light of the impressions carefully created and fostered by writers unacquainted with the true history and sentiments of the two communities and their mutual dependence and their respective heritages. Two such great sections of civilized humanity, thrown together for over a thousand years into intimate contact by the necessities of commerce, industry, social adaptation and political give and take, could not afford to live in perpetual discord. They, therefore, consciously evolved political and social adjustments, almost a cultural synthesis, which, but for the advent of dominating alien rule, might, in the natural course of evolution, have perfected itself by now.[6] It has to be confessed, however, that the relations between the communities have, particularly during the last few years, registered an increasing deterioration. All the same, only a morbidly defeatist mentality can hold, that this deterioration is more than a passing phase, or, that there can be no hope of continuing the existing political union between the two communities in this land and so perfecting it as to eliminate foreign rule and build up a strong independent All India Federation. To permit ourselves to become victims of such, pessimism will be unwise and disastrous. It will amount to turning a deaf ear to those compelling calls for unity and strength, which will not allow themselves to be ignored even in the din of present discords.

Both the communities are followers of great religions, which, like the other great religions of mankind, have a great deal in common. Both still claim allegiance to high ethical codes which have more than a facial resemblance. Fortunately, in India religious cleavage does not run parallel to vital schisms—ethnic, linguistic or cultural.

The tradition of a common past in literature, art, and culture, is still quite alive and can be easily and successfully strengthened by assiduous effort to make it a vital force. The heritage in religion and culture of tolerance and mutual respect, now three thousand years old, can be usefully employed to invigorate the identity which common economic interests establish. On past occasions when internal crisis of disruption threatened the country, Indian civilization proved itself capable of surmounting the danger through compromise and accommodation. The springs of its vitality and renovation are by no means exhausted; indeed they are perennial. The threat of a national catastrophe may yet call forth high moral qualities, compelling a closing of the ranks and a renunciation of differences. What is necessary is a conscious moral effort to extend the bounds of our sympathies, to deepen their foundations, to enlarge and purify our vision and to reinforce the unifying and harmonizing influences which surround us. This is an obligation on all who believe and have faith in the rise of an integrated, strong and independent India, which, by reason of its immense resources has a great part to play in the reconstructed world that is struggling to emerge out of the present chaos.

It will be clear from what is stated above that the view referred to [in the beginning] has presented a distorted picture of Hindu-Muslim relations. It has placed an undue insistence on the things which divide and has ignored the bonds which unite the two communities. The genesis of this British view has to be traced back to the dark events of the Indian Rebellion of 1857, when the foundations of British rule were shaken to their depths by the combination and concerted action of certain important elements of the population. To prevent the recurrence of such a dangerous combination became the chief preoccupation of British policy. The areas, which had misbehaved, were given up as recruiting grounds for the Indian Army; those sections of the population, which were suspected of having taken an active part in the rebellion, had to suffer the full consequences of their misconduct. Those that had remained loyal were favoured. For about thirty years from 1857, the Muslims were in disfavour, because they were suspected of having taken a prominent part in the rebellion. A change, however, came after the foundation of the Indian National Congress in 1885 and its sharp reactions on a great Muslim leader, Sir Syed Ahmad Khan.[7] Originally and for many years a great patriot standing for a united single nation comprising both communities, which he insisted on describing the Hindu Nation, gradually veered round to the view that the right policy for the Muslims, was steadfast loyalty to the British Government and dissociation from all forms of political activity which might bring them into conflict with their Rulers. Barring a few lapses under the influence of exceptional communal excitement or religious emotion, the bulk of the more conservative Muslim leaders had remained faithful to Sir Syed's policy.

Far different has been the history of the activities of non-Muslim leaders. Demand for self-government grew rapidly after the 1885 session of the Indian National Congress. In 1905, Gokhale, a statesman of rare political judgement and realism, asked at the Banaras session of the Congress for the establishment of a system of government in India, similar to that prevailing in the self-governing colonies of the British Empire. The following year, at the Congress session at Calcutta, the veteran Dadabhai Naoroji, demanded '*Swaraj*', a word which, while it fired the imagination of the people, alarmed the British Government to such an extent that prosecutions for sedition, were launched against speakers who used this word. The word *Swaraj*, however, emerged successfully through all these trials and its use as an expression of the ideal of India's political aspirations received high and authoritative recognition in the speech of His late Majesty King George V, at the Delhi Durbar in 1911.

It would have been bad policy if the British Government had placed itself in a position to appear directly in the role of an opponent of Indian self-government. The narrative of the events given below will show how this appearance of direct conflict was avoided.

While Mr. Dadabhai Naoroji was demanding *Swaraj*, a separatist movement on the part of Muslims, of which the full significance was not realized at the time, began to take shape. It has grown steadily and during the last five or six years has attained great force. Sir Syed Ahmad Khan founded the Mohamedan Anglo-Orient College at Aligarh in 1877, which has since developed into the Aligarh Muslim University. The College was not only a seat of western education for Muslim youth, but under the active inspiration and guidance of its first three Principals, Beck, Morison and Archbold, was also a centre of great political activity.[8] Mr. Beck exercised no small influence over Sir Syed Ahmad in bringing about the radical change in latter's political views that took place after the national movement found organized expression in the Indian National Congress.

Mr. Beck and his successors were identified with the later political doctrines of Sir Syed Ahmad, besides being in close touch with the Government of India. After Sir Syed Ahmad's death in 1898, there were influential accessions to Muslims leadership at Aligarh in the persons of Nawab Mohsin-ul-Mulk, and Nawab Vicar-ul-Mulk, who in succession held the office of Secretary of the M.A.O. College. In due course, a very influential deputation was organized, on October 1, 1906.

It is now a matter of common knowledge that this deputation was not altogether spontaneous, but was inspired from Simla. In a letter to Nawab Mohsin-ul-Mulk, dated August 10, 1906, Mr. Archbold, the then Principal of the M.A.O. College, elaborated the idea of this deputation. He also informed the Nawab that the proposals had the blessings of the Government.

Whilst the Muslims, led by Aligarh, had gained a signal triumph, Hindu-India had been deeply agitated over the partition of Bengal in 1905, by which the province was split up in a way which was regarded by the Bengal Hindus as a deliberate attempt to weaken their influence by creating a separate eastern Muslim province. Intense agitation continued from 1907 to 1910, from which Muslims generally held aloof. In 1911, at the King Emperor's Durbar at Delhi, the annulment of the partition of Bengal was announced. This, and the events affecting Islamic kingdoms in the Middle East, created a stir amongst the Muslims and the younger section among them tended to be drawn towards political union with the Hindus.

In October 1916, nineteen elected members of the Indian Legislative Council submitted to the Government of India, a memorandum of proposed reforms.[9] The Muslims put forward their proposals. Their main demands were:

1. The principle of separate representation to be extended to the Punjab and the Central Provinces (previously excluded under the terms of the Act of 1909);
2. Fixation of the number of Muslim seats in the Provincial and Imperial Legislative Councils; and
3. Safeguards against legislation affecting Muslims, their religion and religious usages.

The Lucknow Pact[10] is memorable for many reasons. It showed that Hindus and Muslims could unite to make a common political demand to the British Government. Mutual concessions were made.

Although, the Hindus had, with this hope, agreed to separate electorates for the Muslims, they soon realized that instead of promoting harmony, they had widened the gulf between them and the Muslims. Consequently, during the next few years repeated but unsuccessful attempts were made by means of All Party Conferences and Conventions to bridge this gulf. An important Conference was held in Lucknow in 1928 and a committee was appointed which came to be known as the Nehru Committee.[11] Among its members were Pandit Motilal Nehru (Chairman), Sir Ali Imam and Sir Tej Bahadur Sapru. While making other concessions to the Muslims, the Committee, unlike the framers of the Lucknow Pact, made no concessions to the Muslims on the question of separate electorates. They declared that separate electorates violated the essential principles of responsible government and had "failed to pave the way to a better understanding between the communities". They, therefore, recommended that all elections should be by joint or mixed electorates, and that the only communal safeguards should be reservation of seats, and that too for Muslims only and not for any other community or group, excepting non-Muslims in the North-West Frontier Province. The reservation of seats for Muslims was limited to the Centre and to the province where they were in minority. The right to contest other than reserved seats was to be conceded, but no weightage was to be allowed; the number of seats reserved was to be in strict proportion to the size of the community. "A minority must remain a minority, whether any seats are reserved for it or not." These recommendations, however, did not satisfy the Muslims. So, a further attempt to heal the breach was made by convening a National Convention at Calcutta in December 1928, at which Mahatma Gandhi was present. It, however, broke up without bringing about a settlement.[12]

Dr. Sapru also examined the arguments for and against separate electorates for Muslims and to discuss their effects on the relations between the Hindus and Muslims. As stated above, the first statutory recognition of separate electorates for Muslims was contained in the Act of 1909. The main grounds urged in its favour were that, if Hindus have a voice in the choice of Muslim representatives, only such Muslims will be elected as would be under the influence of Hindus and would not, therefore, satisfactorily represent their community; that in a country like India, divided by race, religion and castes, the only effective safeguard for a community is the right to choose its representatives exclusively from its own members. The main ground, however, on which British authorities have acquiesced in the continuance of separate electorates is that the system has become a settled fact for many years and any attempt to reopen it without the consent of the Muslims would be a breach of faith on the part of the British Government.[13]

Let us examine the argument of settled fact a little more closely. When the Muslim deputation waited on Lord Minto in 1906, the Government of the country was predominantly in British hands. The Legislatures, based on a very narrow franchise, had very limited powers, and their main function was not to control the Executive but to represent to the British Rulers the grievances and wants of the people. The representation by communities had then a plausible basis. But the situation became radically different with the announcement of the policy of carrying India towards responsible government, which since 1919, has been progressively implemented, and with the consequent wide extension of the franchise, Ministers in the provinces are now chosen exclusively from the Legislature and are responsible to it. The Legislature can make and unmake ministries. A Legislature with such wide powers, if constituted on the basis of separate communal electorates, in which one community has no opportunity to influence the choice of the representatives of the other community, creates a permanent majority and minority based exclusively on religion from which there is no escape. The ministry will be composed of men returned, not because they enjoy the suffrages of both communities and, therefore, are under pressure to safeguard the interests of both but, because they are regarded as the most uncompromising champions of the interest of their own community. Such a ministry lends itself to constant attacks both inside and outside the Legislature on grounds of communal bias.

The learned authors of the Montagu Chelmsford Report came unhesitatingly to the conclusion that "the history of self-government among the nations who developed it [responsible government] and spread it through the world is decisively against the admission by the State of any divided allegiance and against the State's arranging its members in any way which encourages them to think of themselves primarily as citizens of any smaller unit than itself." They did not fail to give the warning "division by creeds and classes means the creation of camps organized against each other"—we would add here "on other than national considerations"—"and teaches men to think as partizans and not as citizens and it is difficult to see how the change from this system to national representation is ever to occur". The history of communal representation through separate electorates, particularly the history of the Muslim League, during the twenty five years that have elapsed, is standing testimony to the correctness of judgement of those who were responsible for these observations. That judgement was endorsed wholeheartedly by the Simon Commission. And yet, both in the 1919 and in the 1935 amendments to the Act, separate electorates were not interfered with mainly on the ground that they were a settled fact, any unsettling of which would be condemned by the Muslims as amounting to the withdrawal of the valued privilege which had been accorded to them in 1906. The problem of choosing the members of responsible ministries in the provinces from legislatures based on separate communal electorates had to be squarely faced in 1935 with the prospect of the advent of provincial autonomy, but beyond recommending a minor amendment to the Instrument of Instructions to Governors, the Joint Parliamentary Committee evaded the only satisfactory solution of it in the hope that in the future, parties may develop in the Provincial Legislatures which would cut across communal lines". The actual development has, however, been in the case of the Muslims, the rise and growth of a frankly communal Party, in the Legislature and outside, which has claimed and obtained from responsible authorities the right, in legislative debate and political negotiations outside, not merely a status of political equality with national political parties and organizations but even to demand that no Muslim who does not belong to it but belongs to a nationally organized party can be considered a representative of his community.

In the only election that has been so far held since the inauguration of provincial responsible governments in 1937, the Congress alone sought the suffrage of the electorate as a national party. The Congress candidates, relying for their success on their powerful Party organization, on the immense influence of Mahatma Gandhi and on the energy and drive of their leaders, made no communal approach to the electorate, but based their appeal on the interests of the masses. On the other hand, the Muslim League, though it had not assumed its present militant role as the sole representative of all Muslims could make no such appeal, with the result that the number of avowed Leaguers returned was small. The communal bitterness that was engendered by these results and more particularly by the exclusion of Leaguers from the Ministries formed in the Congress majority provinces, has increased to such an extent that the cry has gone forth from the Muslim League that —the Muslims must form their own separate State. Every extension of the franchise will only increase the evil if communities have to vote in watertight compartments. If, on a decline of the influence of Congress ideals at any future date, the Indian elections are fought on a purely communal ticket, only fanatics of both the communities will be returned, who will make good government impossible. Recent experience has shown that communal electorates will make the task of forming governments on the basis of political parties almost impossible. Ministries be constantly exposed to pressure to make them more communal. The recent struggle between the Muslim League and the Union Ministry in the Punjab is a striking example of this tendency. Every election will become an arena of mutual vilification of Hindus and Muslims and the minorities will be at the complete mercy of a permanent majority of extremists. What was once regarded as a necessary means for the protection of minority interests, is fast becoming a potent cause of mutual hatred and suspicion, keeping the two communities increasingly apart.

The contagion has already spread over Municipalities, District Boards and other local bodies. It has fed the desire that in every organization, for example, Chambers of Commerce, labour organizations and even universities, Muslims should have separate electorates. Suggestions are not wanting that, in the name of the peace and tranquility of India, this division should be carried down to every village and hamlet.

The contagion is likewise spreading to the Indian States as legislative and other popular elected bodies come to be established. This could not have been anticipated when separate electorates were first established in British India. It is almost certain that, if communal electorates persisted in British India, they will become common in course of time in the Indian States with results no less disastrous.

Another argument is that the Hindus agreed to separate electorates in 1916, and, that they have, therefore, no right to condemn them now. If there is to be a change, it is argued, it must be by common consent. We have already pointed out [above] that Hindu leaders like Tilak and Muslim leaders like Jinnah, regarded separate electorates as temporary. In the Conferences, one held in 1925 and the other in 1928, Mr. Jinnah was prepared to settle the Hindu-Muslim question on the basis of joint electorates. In 1927, speaking from the League platform he said: "I am not wedded to separate electorates, although I must say that the overwhelming majority of the Mussalmans firmly and honestly believe that it is the only method by which they can be sure."[14]

Even as late as 1931, addressing the U.P. Muslim Conference, held at Allahabad on August 8, Mr. Jinnah said: "The next question that arises is one of separate *versus* joint electorates. As most of you know, if a majority is conceded in the Punjab and Bengal, I would personally prefer a settle merit on the basis of joint electorates."[15]

Sir Muhmmad Shafi was prepared to agree to joint electorates in 1932, during the meetings of the Minorities Sub-Committee of the Round Table Conference, provided that the Hindus were prepared to make certain concessions. It can be inferred from these pronouncements of Muslim leaders that, till not very long ago, several of their outstanding representatives were prepared to abandon separate electorates for a *quid pro quo*. Unfortunately, however, the attitude of the British Government in this vital matter has been halting and cynical and has given room for the not unreasonable suspicion that they desired to stereotype divisions so as "to preserve undisturbed and indisputable the fabric of British Power".

The unreserved condemnation of separate electorates in principle and on the merits by their spokesmen, coupled with their maintenance in fact stamps this attitude as hypocritical, a charge which, nearly thirty years ago, the 'Montagu Chelmsford Report warned the Government, would be made and which it would find very difficult to meet...'

Dr. Sapru was unreservedly of opinion that separate electorates have been the curse of Indian politics for nearly forty years and that unless they are abolished the achievement of independence or full self-government must continue to remain a dream. The settled fact must be unsettled. But for the decision (pledge as it has sometimes been described) in 1906, the authoritative pronouncements have made it clear, a different policy would have been adopted long ago. That decision was confessedly a mistaken and, wrong one, however deliberately it may have been taken. No Government, which is not merely in power but accepts active responsibility for right decisions, can legitimately flinch from the task of righting a manifestly wrong decision which, though nearly forty years old, has been so mischievous in its effects.

REFERENCES

1. *Sapru-Radhakrishnan Letters*, Sapru Papers deposited in the Government of India, National Library, *op. cit.*
2. Report Vol. I - Survey (1930), p. 25.
3. Session 1933-34, Vol. I (Part I); Report, p. 1.
4. *Constitutional Problem in India*, 1944, p. 31.
5. Beni Prasad, *Hindu-Muslim Questions* (Lahore: Minerva), 1943, p. 7.
6. Patwardhan, *Triangle* (Bombay: Padma Publishers), 1967, p. 18.
7. *Ibid.*
8. *Ibid.*
9. Das, Durga, *Curzon to Nehru and After* (New York: John Dobu), 1970, p. 57.
10. *Ibid.*
11. *Constitutional Proposals of the Sapru Committee*, 1945.
12. Das, Durga, *Curzon to Nehru, op. cit.*, pp. 154-5.
13. Report on Indian Constitutional Reforms (Montagu-Chelmsford), paras 227-31.
14. Ambedkar, B.R., *Pakistan* (Bombay: Thacker & Co.), 1945, p. 314.
15. *Ibid.*, p. 315.

6

SOCIO-ECONOMIC IDEAS

Neither political pursuits nor a crowded legal career could keep so versatile a mind as Sapru's completely pre-occupied. He was all the time making impressive sallies into other fields and pastures, new fields which did not necessarily belong to a constitutional lawyer. The country's varied problems other than legal and political, were claiming his earnest attention. These problems were mainly socio-economic whose solution, according to the veteran thinker, should be attempted side by side with the struggle for political emancipation. Some of his ideas on these vital problems can be gleaned from his many convocation addresses at the universities and colleges. With his experience of the working of the universities he could do some deep personal thinking on the problems of education in their academic as well as vocational aspects. His convocation addresses are brilliant exercises in educational exploration. They are never trite or platitudinous. His ideas are sharp, clear and down to earth, some of which are relevant even to the vastly changed current context. No wonder! he was very much in demand for delivering convocation addresses.

One of the points that emerges from these addresses is that Sapru wanted each university to develop a personality of its own, depending on the local conditions, resources and other factors. Each of them should also specialize in a particular discipline, he felt. Also there must be thoroughness and depth in the study of such subjects as Medicine and Engineering about which Sapru was very insistent.

On whether university education had been a success in our country, Sapru made a few points at the Lucknow University. While as a result of English education eminent persons had come up in different fields, like Science, History, Economics and so on, the national average was, in his opinion, "deplorably Low."[1] This was because for the vast majority of the students it was not academic excellence but the degree that mattered. This was one of the recurrent themes of several of his convocation addresses. As early as in 1925 the idea came to his mind that degrees for the sake of a job should be discouraged, otherwise the time was not distant when there would be such a mad rush for university degrees as to create a sheer pressure of numbers and a steep fall in the standards of education leading to an increasing unemployment and a devaluation of education itself. As education spread and the employment prospects grew more and more dim, there was the resultant discontent and frustration, specially in the thirties. Sapru became fully convinced that the only remedy was a radical change in the education system. His Allahabad University convocation address of 1933 is a fine discourse on the economics of employment. Fully appreciative that academic learning "rises superior to the consideration of a utilitarian character", Sapru however painfully realized that the call of hunger was more insistent than the call of culture and he had no alternative but to plead for "practical and scientific education, an education which will enable us to stand the stress of modern competitive life."[2] His emphasis on vocational education was unqualified and unrelaxing, seeing that the universities, were turning out "hungry crowds of middle class graduates", disowned alike, by the Government and the society.

Sapru wanted work oriented education, an education that makes for profession and career, not an ivory tower education of a purely cultural content. He would have a large number of students diverted to vocational training or training in agricultural pursuits where possible, so that the students could straightway get settled down in life. Higher education should be available only to those students who were likely to benefit by it, and for the rest of them education should be vocationalized. At the Patna University convocation, he said that secondary education should be self-sufficient and not subservient to university education.[3]

By 1935 the economic situation deteriorated further leading to acute unemployment among the educated and grave political unrest. Greatly disturbed by this development Sapru spoke at the Patna University convocation:

> "... I cannot reconcile myself of India becoming a nation of learned beggars".[4] On the strength of his Western experience he declared that education must be viewed as connected with employment and that, for the vast majority of students who were not likely to benefit by higher education, the only course left open was vocational, industrial or some other employment oriented education.

All this may create the impression that Sapru was averse to the cultural aspect of education. But that was not so. Himself a fine product of a cultural synthesis, Sapru was not a Philistine in his outlook on culture. But the compulsions of the situation was such as to force his attention down to earth to take, by and large, an utilitarian view of the matter. The serious economic crisis and the mounting problems of educated unemployment were serious matters for a pragmatic politician like Sapru quietly to pass by.

Sapru's views on the medium of education are quite unambiguous. He was firmly of the opinion that a foreign language could not serve as a medium of instruction. One's own Culture could not be developed through a foreign language, he felt. Nevertheless, while addressing the Lucknow University convocation in 1925, he said: "... there are subjects which must continue to be taught through the medium of English for a long time to come until at any rate the pioneer work in our language has been done."[5] His protest was "not against the use of English or the study of the English literature but against the neglect which has been allowed to overtake our languages."[6]

Could university education serve any social purpose? Sapru's reply would definitely be in the affirmative. Although he prescribed vocational education for the vast bulk of the students, he was however not impervious to the values of academic learning. Sapru would like the students to imbibe through their academic education "a genuine spirit of broad toleration"[7] which, he thought, was the need of the hour. Secondly, such an education should create in the students "an evangelical zeal for Indian Unity."[8] Sapru could well see how healthy nationalism was being sought to be distorted by communalism and how various fissiparous and parochial trends were seeking to vitiate the modern progressive conception of a new India. He wanted liberal academic education to mould the students into a national force.

The report of the United Provinces Committee on Unemployment is one more testimony to Sapru's deep understanding of the country's socio-economic problems normally having nothing to do with his specific field of constitutional scholarship and advocacy. Appointed by the Governor of the Province in October 1934, the Committee had Sapru as Chairman and seven other eminent personalities as members. Perhaps the Governor could not have made a better choice of the Chairman. The Committee issued a questionnaire, toured various centres, recorded evidence and collected masses of materials from various sources, both Indian and foreign. The result was a voluminous report of about 400 pages of great depth and understanding which may claim to be a remarkable work of its kind. It redounds greatly to the dynamism of its Chairman that the report could be completed in an astonishingly short period of time—a little over a year. The report was signed in December 1935 and released in January 1936. Even after a lapse of four decades, many of its contents remain refreshingly relevant.

Sapru did not approach his task in a conventional way. He utilized his stay in Europe by studying the problem in a comparative manner. He talked to the representatives of the League of Nations and the International Labour Office about education and employment and also examined the working of the London County Council in this regard. He was thus in possession of an enormous volume of materials to work upon. Sapru personally did herculean labour. The part played by him was so conspicuous that the other members of the Committee deemed it fit to add a note to the report expressing their gratitude to the Chairman "for his inestimable services in collecting most valuable information for the Committee in India and Europe and for the immense labour undertaken at a great personal sacrifice in preparing the draft of the report for the consideration of the Committee".[9]

So far as unemployment was concerned, the Committee came to the general conclusion that "the situation has been steadily deteriorating over the last 10 or 15 years and that during the last five years in particular the problem has become increasingly acute."[10] Having made a review of the education system and the scope of employment in Government service, Industry, Agriculture, Engineering, Commerce etc., the Committee made some very important recommendations whose connotations far transcended the provincial limits.

The Committee argued that the Education portfolio had already been in Indian hands and that it would be more so with the ushering in of the new Act. There should therefore be no difficulty in overhauling the education system so that, while giving the free opportunity for the development of knowledge and culture, it might at the same time make young men practical and vocationally equipped.

On primary education the Committee observed that it should aim not only at literacy but also at making the pupils useful in the rural context. The Committee therefore recommended that primary education which should be compulsory and of six years duration should have a bias towards rural occupation. So far as secondary education was concerned the Committee's view was that it should have two kinds of certificates, one qualifying the pupils for the science and the humanities course and another for the vocational courses which incidentally should be diversified and based more and more on practical training.

University education was a more complex field. The Committee did not intend to fix any arbitrary limit on admission to the universities which was definitely on the increase. Nevertheless it suggested that there should be greater strictness exercised in the matter of admission."[11] It laid an unerring emphasis on scientific and vocational education. Further it favoured research work of practical utility and a liaison between the Universities' Science faculties and Trade and Industry. Another important suggestion was about the need of having an agency for the placement of the trained personnel, something equivalent to the present day employment exchanges. Indeed it suggested an employment guidance authority for this purpose.

The Committee had to grapple with another serious problem that is, unemployment among the Law graduates. Greatly concerned over the deteriorating condition of the profession, the Committee remarked: "The legal profession in these Provinces is far too crowded with the consequence that there is a great deal of unemployment in it."[12] The Committee envisaged two distinctly different types of functions for different classes of lawyers, something approximating to the institution of solicitorship. One class was to do the advocacy and another class, the preparatory work, namely, drafting, conveyancing and so on. The Committee would have a more diversified legal education, covering subjects till then neglected and also more Law teachers on a more adequate pay. It insisted on a three-year Law degree course and recommended the setting up of a Council of Legal Education.

Vitally interested in the profession of law, Sapru was pained to see unemployment among the Law graduates as much as he was anxious to see that the standards of the profession were maintained. At the Punjab University convocation he spoke of the "mass production of Law graduates" and suggested a commission for the reorganization of the profession.[13] He had a very high conception of Law. At the convocation of Sri Pratap College of Srinagar on July 5, 1940, he described Law as 'an organic science permeating every aspect of human life.',[14] From the academic angle he advocated a comparative study of the subject, as he himself had so profoundly done.

The Committee traversed the whole field of employment like Agriculture, Industry, Medicine, Commerce and so on and explored subsidiary fields like Pharmacy, Dentistry, Librarianship, Architecture etc. making suitable recommendations regarding all these. It suggested the till then novel idea of research in educational psychology and scientific career counselling as obtaining in the Western countries.

When the report came up for discussion in the U. P. Legislative Council in March 1936, Sapru, though not a member, was present in the House on an invitation from the Governor. He pleaded for adequate funds for the implementation of the recommendations. About the same time his son Mr. P.N. Sapru moved a resolution in the Council of State urging the implementation of the Committee report on an all India level and drew appreciative official response.[15] Relevant to U.P. the report assumed an all-India importance. The *Modern Review* editorially noted that since the problem was similar all over the country, "both the Governments and the people of the Provinces outside the Provinces of Agra and Oudh should make full use of the labours of the Sapru Committee."[16]

The main crux of his socio-economic ideas can be seen in his evidence before the Age of Consent Committee[17] in the form of questions and answers which follow as under:

Q. Can you suggest any method by which a vast number of orthodox people would be permitted to have pre-puberty marriages which they look upon as essential and yet postpone consummation effectually beyond sixteen or eighteen?

Sapru: My method is one of undisguised warfare against the orthodox people.

Q. Can you suggest any other remedy by which the two views could possibly be reconciled?

Sapru: Absolutely irreconcilable. You cannot reconcile common sense with the *shastras* or with the orthodox books on religion. That is my honest opinion.

Q. Suppose a law is passed permitting marriages at an early age, pre-puberty or otherwise, but enjoining that a girl shall not be sent to her father-in-law's house till she completes her sixteenth year and imposing a fine for breaking the law, do you think that in that case we can achieve our object?

Sapru: I believe it is possible provided Government has the substantial police forces in India and post a policeman in every orthodox house.

Q. Do you in fact think that this is not feasible?

Sapru: Absolutely infeasible. But even if a girl is enjoined not to go to her father-in-law's house before the prescribed age, and if the law is broken what is the penalty that you are going to impose?

Q. The penalty will be fine or imprisonment. Will that not do?

Sapru: So far as fine is concerned, well, I believe most of the orthodox people will much sooner pay the fine than forego their orthodox views. So far as the question of punishment is concerned, I am willing to support the Committee provided a very severe penalty of imprisonment for the father, father-in-law, mother, mother-in-law and for the husband is given. Nothing short of that, I would agree to.

Mr. Yakub: What punishment would you suggest?

Sapru: Five years' imprisonment.

Q. Is that the only way by which you can bring a rule into force in this country? Will you not also give whipping to the boy ?

Sapru: I have no compulsion in regard to this matter and I will be still more severe if the husband happens to be a graduate or an undergraduate of any University.

Q. Do you think that Government or the Legislature would be justified in legislating upon a matter of this kind which is a social or socio religious question?

Sapru: I think that there is ample justification both for the Legislature and for the Government to legislate upon a matter of this kind, but I am not prepared to credit the Legislature or the Government with the necessary amount of courage to undertake it.

Q. Do you think that the Government should legislate for instance in the matter of prohibiting drinks ?

Sapru: I am an absolute opponent of prohibition.

Q. How do you distinguish between the two cases? One is as bad and evil as the other?

Sapru: I don't think that the evil is of the same character or of the same extent. Amongst the 350 millions of people you will find that the number who drink is comparatively very much smaller than the number of parents who get their girls married at the age of ten or eleven.

Evidence viii, p. 248. No. 4.

Mrs. Nehru: Do you think that it is impossible to bring about any reform by terrorism, specially when the majority of the people are orthodox?

Sapru: It is not a question of terror to my mind, but it is a question of strength. If the Government is prepared to face some silly questions which arise in the course of our national life why should not the Government take a bold step in this?

Q. But where a democratic Government is concerned and the majority of people are orthodox, is it possible?

Sapru: But you cannot have a truly democratic Government so long as the people are orthodox. That is my conviction.

Q. I suppose you know a great deal about Turkey. Can you tell us how those social laws are administered there?

Sapru: Personally speaking I am a great admirer of Turkey and the Turkish statesmen. When I travelled there, I saw many schools and colleges where girls are educated. I think the girls' schools there might be favourably compared with some girls' Schools that I saw in England and France. The girls are absolutely free. There are a number of girls employed in the post offices, in the banks and in the public offices. They are extremely dignified girls and very well behaved. All these things were brought about in the case of the Turks, although the majority of them never agreed to all these reforms, because there was one strong man at the helm of affairs who thought that his policy should be carried out, and he never shrunk from the consequences.

Q. What methods did he adopt to bring about those reforms when the majority of the people did not agree with his point of view?

Sapru: I think it was by sheer force.

Mr. Mitra: In the law of marriage are you ready to provide exemptions?

Sapru : No.

Q. You certainly think that there are some orthodox people who sincerely believe that according to the *shastras* they should have pre-puberty marriages?

Sapru: I don't dispute their sincerity or their existence, but I regret it.

Q. Are you not ready to make any special provision for them?

Sapru: No.

Q. Don't you think that those orthodox people who are in a majority will resent this marriage law and will try to resist it?

Sapru: I have no doubt they will resist it and they have resented during these 2,000 years.

Q. Shouldn't their resentment take some serious shape?

Sapru: If it takes a serious shape, Government should be prepared to put it down.

Mr. Shah Nawaz: Do you think that women have been so far the victims of these social evils?

Sapru: I think so.

Q. Do you think that fixing the minimum marriageable age will be one of the first steps towards their emancipation ?

Sapru : It will be one of the steps but I won't say it will be a very big step.

Evidence viii, p. 250. No. 6.

Q. What is the opinion of the women from countryside, so far as the orthodox women are concerned?

Sapru: There is not much to choose between them and the orthodox men.

Q. Don't you think that some orthodox Brahmins in their heart of hearts feel that this is a tremendous evil, viz., early marriage and early consummation?

Sapru: Well, if they feel like that, then I can say they are not orthodox. They are insincere.

Q. Do you think that all the orthodox men are insincere?

Sapru: If you ask my candid opinion I believe at least sixty per cent of the so called orthodox men are insincere.

Q. Is it not a fact that people do not know the evil effects of early marriage, therefore they have recourse to early marriage?

Sapru: They have known it for generations, but they have not the courage to act upon it... An ordinary graduate understands it, and my grudge is against the ordinary graduate.

Q. What are your reasons for fixing the age of marriage at eighteen ?

Sapru: Because I believe that in this country physically girls do not arrive at maturity before the age of eighteen. I should give them time to acquire more knowledge and experience.

Q. I don't think you can visualise the period when every girl will be able to read in college?

Sapru: I do emphatically when every girl ordinarily will be decently educated.

Q. So far as physical development is concerned, doctors are unanimous that at sixteen there will be no physical injury to the girl or her progeny. Would you be satisfied if sixteen is fixed as a first step?

Sapru: I beg to differ from these medical men. They may be sound medically, but socially they are absolutely wrong.

Evidence viii, p. 252. No. 9.

Q. If there is provision for occupation of their minds and if the Government provides compulsory education then you would recommend marriage at eighteen and not before that?

Sapru : Compulsory education or no compulsory education, the nation should not be allowed to further deteriorate.

Q. The lawgivers recommend sixteen ?

Sapru : My answer is, make a bonfire of these lawgivers. These lawgivers are at the root of our downfall. I have no respect for any such lawgiver.

Q. May I know that you want as little interference with the social and religious customs of the people as possible?

Sapru : I want as much interference in their religious views as possible provided you have got a national Government or even foreign Government which is national in its outlook.

Q. Do you think there will be great discontent in the country if the Government does not make any legislation fixing the age of marriage ?

Sapru: So far as the bulk of the educated people are concerned, I think there is not much to choose between them and the orthodox people ... They are prepared to rebel against other things but not against their social system. That is my idea of my educated compatriots.

Q. You complain that educated people do not do any work or propaganda with regard to this evil?

Sapru : They fight shy of their intellectual convictions.

REFERENCES

1. *Lucknow University Convocation Address,* November 7, 1925.
2. *Allahabad University Convocation Address,* December 16, 1933.
3. *Patna University Convocation Address,* November 30, 1935.
4. *Ibid.*
5. *Lucknow University Convocation Address,* November 7, 1925.
6. *Ibid.*
7. *Ibid.*
8. *Allahabad University Convocation Address,* December 16, 1933.
9. *Report of the United Provinces Committee on Unemployment.*
10. *Ibid.*
11. *Ibid.*
12. *Ibid.*
13. *Panjab University Convocation Address,* December 2, 1936.
14. Address at the *Sri Pratap College Convocation,* 1940.
15. Council of State Debates, *Indian Annual Register,* Vol. V, 1936.
16. *Modern Review,* Feburary 1936.
17. T.B. Sapru's Oral Statement before Age of Consent Committee made on January 16, 1929, at Allahabad.

BIBLIOGRAPHY

Address at the Sri Pratap College Convocation, 1940.

Aiyar, S.P. (ed.), *The Politics of Mass Violence in India* (Bombay: P.C. Manaktala & Sons), 1967.

Allahabad University Convocation Address, December 16, 1933.

Ambedkar, B.R., *Pakistan* (Bombay: Thacker & Co.), 1946.

Ambedkar, B.R., *What Congress and Gandhi Have Done to the Untouchables* (Bombay: Thacker & Co.), 1946.

Ambirajan, S., *Political Economy and Monetary Management in India,* 1766-1914 (Madras: Affiliated East-West Press), 1984.

Azad, Maulana Abul Kalam, *India Wins Freedom* (Madras: Orient Longman), 1989.

Bannerjee, A.K., *Aspects of Indo British Economic Relations,* 1858-1898 (Bombay: Oxford University Press), 1982.

Bannerjee, Arun, *Finances in the Early Raj: Investments and the External Sector* (New Delhi: Sage Publications), 1995.

Bannerjee, S.N., *A Nation in Making* (London: Milford), 1925.

Bar Council of Delhi, *Commemoration Volume* (compiled and published on the occasion of the Birth Centenary of Dr. Tej Bahadur Sapru), Bar Council of Delhi & Indian Council of World Affairs, New Delhi.

Bell Charles, *Indian Mutiny* (London: Clarendon Press), 1931.

Beni Prasad, *Hindu-Muslim Questions* (Lahore: Minerva), 1943.

Besant Annie, *How India Wrought for Freedom: The Story of Indian National Congress* (New Delhi: Michiko Panjathan), 1975.

Bimal Prasad (ed.), *A Revolutionary Quest* (Delhi: Oxford University Press), 1980.

Black, R.D., *Collison, Economic Thought and the Irish Question, 1817-1870* (Cambridge: Cambridge University Press), 1960.

Bose, S.K., *Tej Bahadur Sapru* (New Delhi: Publications Division, Ministry of Information and Broadcasting, Government of India), 1978.

Bose, Subhas Chandra, *The Indian Struggle* (Calcutta: Published for Netaji Publishing Society), 1948.

Broadcast Talk, All India Radio, Lucknow, December 8, 1941, published under *T.C. Miscellany* in Twentieth Century, January 1942.

Buch, M.A., *The Rise and Growth of Indian Liberalism* (Baroda: the auth), 1938.

Chandra, B., M. Mukerjee, A. Mukerjee, K.N. Panikkar and S. Mahajan, *India's Struggle for Independence 1857-1947* (New Delhi: Penguin Books), 1989.

Chandra, Bipan, *Communalism in India* (New Delhi: Vani Educational Books), 1984.

Chandra, Bipin *et al.*, *India's Struggle for Independence, 1857-1947* (New Delhi: Penguin Books), 1989.

Chandra, Bipan, *Modern India* (New Delhi: NCERT), 1976.

Chandra, Bipan, *Nationalism and Colonialism in Modern India* (New Delhi: Orient Longman), 1979.

Chandra, Bipan, *The Rise and Growth of Economic Nationalism in India, Economic Policies of Indian National Leadership 1880-1905* (New Delhi: People's Publishing House), 1966.

Charlesworth, Neil, *British Rule and the Indian Economy, 1800-1914* (London: Macmillan), 1982.

Chintamani, C.Y., *Indian Politics Since Mutiny* (Allahabad: Kitabistan), 1947.

Chintamani, C.Y., "The Provincial Conferences of Allahabad", *Modern Review,* May 1907.

Chirol, Valentine, *India, Old and New* (New Delhi: Lights and Life Publications), 1975.

Chirol, Valentine, *The Indian Unrest* (New Delhi: Lights and Life Publications), 1979.

Coase, R.H., *Essays on Economics and Economists* (Chicago: The University of Chicago Press), 1994.

Collins, Larry and Lapierre, Dominique, *Freedom at Midnight* (New Delhi: Vikas Publishing House), 1997.

Constitutional Problem in India, 1944.

Constitutional Proposals of the Sapru Committee, 1945.

Council of State Debates, Indian Annual Register, Vol. V, 1936.

Dalton, Dennis, *Indian Idea of Freedom* (New Delhi: Manohar), 1982.

Das, Durga, *Curzon to Nehru and After* (New York: John Dobu), 1970.

Dasgupta, Ajit K., *A History of Indian Economic Thought* (London: Routledge), 1993.

Datta, V.N., *Madan Lal Dhingra and the Revolutionary Movement* (New Delhi: Vikas Publishing House), 1978.

Dawarkadas, *India's Fight for Freedom: An Eye-witness Story, 1913-37* (Bombay: Popular Prakashan), 1960.

Desai, A.R., *Social Background of Indian Nationalism* (Bombay: Popular Prakashan), 1976.

Dharamvira, *Lala Hardayal and Revolutionary Movements of His Times* (New Delhi: Indian Book Company), 1970.

Dutt, Iswara K., *The Street of Ink* (London: John Arden), 1955.

Fifty Years with Sir Tej Bahadur Sapru, *Hindustan Review,* March, 1949.

Gandhi, M.K., *An Autobiography or The Story of My Experiments with Truth* (Ahmedabad: Navajivan Publishing House), 1983.

Gandhi, M.K., *Hind Swaraj* (Ahmedabad: Navajivan Publishing House), 1983.

Georgescu-Roegen, Nicholas, *Analytical Economics: Issues and Problems* (Cambridge, Massachusetts: Harvard University Press), 1966.

Ghosh, Kalicharan, *The Roll of Honours: Ancedotes of Indian Martyrs* (Calcutta: Vidya Baharati), 1975.

Gooch, G.P., *Nationalism* (London: Longman), 1945.

Gopal, S. (ed.), *Selected Works of Jawaharlal Nehru,* Second Series, Vol. 4 (New Delhi: Jawaharlal Nehru Memorial Fund), 1986.

Gopal, S. (ed.), *Selected Works of Jawaharlal Nehru,* Second Series, Vol. 5 (New Delhi: Jawaharlal Nehru Memorial Fund), 1987.

Guha, A.C., *First Spark of Revolution* (Delhi: Orient Longman), 1972.

Hardayal, *Hints for Self Culture* (Delhi: Rajkamal Publications), 1948.

Holmes, T.R., *History of Indian Mutiny* (London: Macmillan), 1898.

Hindustan Review Enters its Fiftieth Year, *Hindustan Review,* July 1949.

In Memorium, the late Jogdra Nath Choudhry, Allahabad High Court Centenary Commemoration, Vol. I.

Indian Annual Register, Vol. I, 1931.

Indian Legislative Council Proceedings, February 2, 1917.

Indian Legislative Council Proceedings, September 7, 1918.

Jayakar, M.R., *The Story of My Life,* 2 Volumes (Bombay: Asia Publishing House), 1958.

Jog, N.C., *Lokamanya Bal Gangadhar Tilak* (New Delhi: Publications Division, Ministry of Information & Broadcasting, Government of India), 1990.

Joshi, V.C., *Sri Aurobindo—An Interpretation* (New Delhi: Vikas Publishers), 1973.

Jayakar Papers, File No. 454, Letter 80, May 8, 1931 (New Delhi: Nation Archiver)

Katju, K.N., *Reminiscences and Experiments in Advocacy* (Allahabad: Kitabistan), 1956.

Keer, Dhananjay, *Veer Savarkar* (Bombay: Popular Prakashan), 1966.

Keith, A.B., *A Constitutional History of India* (London: Methuen), 1937.

Ker, James Campbell, *Political Trouble in India* (Calcutta: Superintendent Government Printing), 1917.

Kumar, Mohan, *Sir Tej Bahadur Sapru: A Political Biography* (Gwalior: Vipul Prakashan), 1981.

Kunzuru in Commemoration Volume, New Delhi, 1976.

Kurdas, Cigdern, "The Whig Historian on Adam Smith: Paul Samuelson's Canonical Model", *History of Economics Society Bulletin,* X. 1 (Spring), 1988.

Lakatos, Imre, "Falsification and the Methodology of Scientific Research Programmes" in *Criticism and the Growth of Knowledge,* edited by Imre Lakatos and Alan Musgrave (Cambridge: Cambridge University Press), 1970.

Laski, Harold, *Grammar of Politics* (London: Allen), 1948.

Low, D.A., "The Government of India and the First Non-Cooperation Movement 1920-22", *Journal of Asian Studies,* Vol. XXV, 1966.

Low, D.A., "Rearguard Action: Selected Essays on Late Colonial Indian History", Asian Studies Association of Australia, South Asian Publications Series No. 10 (New Delhi: Sterling Publishers Pvt. Ltd.), 1966.

Low, D.A., *Britain and Indian Nationalism: The Imprint of Ambiguity 1929-1942* (Cambridge: Cambridge University Press), 1997.

Lucknow University Convocation Address, November 7, 1925.

Majumdar, R.C. (Gen. ed.), "Struggle for Freedom", *History and Culture of the Indian People Series,* Vol. 11 (Bombay: Bharatiya Vidya Bhawan), 1969.

Manuscript of a short biography of Dr. Tej Bahadur Sapru by late Justice P.N. Sapru (unpublished).

Masani, R.P., *Dadabhai Naoroji: The Grand Old Man of India* (London: George Allen and Unwin Ltd.), 1939.

Masani, R.P., *Dadabhai Naoroji* (New Delhi: Publications Division, Government of India), 1960.

Masselos, Jim, *Indian Nationalism: A History* (New Delhi: Sterling), 1985.

Mathur, B.D., *Gokhale—A Political Biography* (Bombay: Himalaya Publishers), 1955.

McCarthy, Justin, *History of Our Times,* Vol. II (London: Chatts), 1897.

Mead, Henery, *The Sepoy Revolt: Its Causes & Consequences* (Delhi: Gyan), 1986.

Michael, Brecher, *Nehru—A Political Biography* (London: London Press), 1959.

Mill, John Stuart, *Principles of Political Economy,* edited by W.J. Ashley (London: Longmans, Green and Co.), 1909.

Modern Review, February 1936.

Mody, Homi, *Pherozeshah Mehta* (New Delhi: Publications Division, Ministry of Information & Broadcasting, Government of India), 1963.

Moore, R.J., *Liberalism and Indian Politics 1872-1922* (London: Edward Arnold), 1966.

Moore, R.J., *The Crisis of Indian Unity: 1917-1940* (New Delhi: Oxford University Press), 1974.

Mukherjee, Tapan, "Theory of Economic Drain: Impact of British Rule on the Indian Economy: 1840-1900" in *Economic Imperialism: A Book of Readings*, edited by K.E. Boulding and Tapan Mukherjee (Ann Arbor: The University of Michigan Press), 1972.

Nabers, Lawrence, "The Positive and Genetic Approaches" in *The Structure of Economic Science Essays on Methodology*, edited by Sherman Roy Krupp (Englewood Cliffs, N.J.: Prentice Hall, Inc.), 1966.

Nanda, B.R., *Gandhi, Pan-Islamism, Imperialism and Nationalism in India* (Bombay: Oxford University Press), 1989.

Nanda, B.R. (ed.), *Selected Works of Gobind Ballabh Pant,* Vol.I (New Delhi: Oxford University Press), 1993.

Nanda, B.R., *The Making of a Nation: India's Road to Independence* (New Delhi: Harper Collins India Pvt. Ltd.), 1998.

Naoroji, Dadabhai, *Speeches and Writings of Dadabhai Naoroji* (Madras:G.A. Natesan & Co.), n.d.

Naoroji, Dadabhai, *Essays, Speeches, Addresses and Writings* (Bombay: Caxton Printing Works), 1899.

Naoroji, Dadabhai, *Poverty and Un-British Rule in India* (New Delhi: Publications Division, Government of India), 1962.

Nehru, Jawaharlal, *An Autobiography* (London: The Bodley Head), 1958.

Ohdedar, A.K., *The Sapru Correspondence—A Checklist* (First Series) (Calcutta: National Library, Government of India), 1961.

Pandey, B.N., *The Break-up of British India* (London: Macmillan & Co.), 1969.

Pandey, B.N. (ed.), *The Indian National Movement 1850-1947—Select Documents* (London: Macmillan & Co.), 1979.

Panikar, K.M., *His Highness the Maharaja of Bikaner* (Bombay Asia), 1955.

Panjab University Convocation Address, December 2, 1936.

Parliamentary Papers, House of Commons, Vol. III.

Parmanand, Bhai, *The Story of My Life* (New Delhi: S. Chand), 1982.

Parekh, Bhikhu, *Colonialism, Tradition and Reform* (Delhi: Sage Publications), 1999.

Parvate, T.V., *Gopal Krishna Gokhale* (Ahmedabad: Navajivan Publishing House), 1959.

Patna University Convocation Address, November 30, 1935.

Patwardhan, *Triangle* (Bombay: Padma Publishers), 1967.

Philips, C.H. (ed.), *The Evolution of India and Pakistan 1858-1947 Select Documents* (London: George Allen & Unwin), 1962.

Presidential Address, First United Province of Agra and Oudh Lawyer's Conference, Allahabad, 6-7, November, 1938

Proceedings of the First Round Table Conference.

Rai, Lala Lajpat, *The Story of My Life* (New Delhi: D.A.V. Publications), 1987.

Rai, Lala Lajpat, *Young India: An Interpretation and a History of the Nationalist Movement from Within* (New Delhi: Publications Division, Ministry of Information & Broadcasting, Government of India), 1968.

Raina (ed.), *Welding the Nation* (Bombay: N.M. Tripathi Pvt. Ltd.), 1976.

Raina (ed.), *Tej Bahadur Sapru—Responsa: Selected Legal Opinions* (Bombay: N.M. Tripathi Pvt. Ltd.), 1976.

Raina, K.N. and V. Gopala Ratnam (eds.), *Tej Bahadur Sapru: Profiles and Tributes* (Allahabad: The Indian Press Pvt. Ltd.), 1971.

Raina, K.N. and K.V. Gopala Ratnam, *Recollections and Impressions* (Allahabad: The Indian Press Pvt. Ltd.), 1971.

Rajendra Prasad, *An Autobiography* (Bombay: Asia Publishing House), 1957.

Ranade, Mahadev Govind, *Ranade's Economic Writings,* edited by Bipan Chandra (New Delhi: Gian Publishing House), 1990.

Reddy, P.L. Sanjeev and Mishra, S.N. (eds.), *Sardar Vallabhbhai Patel: The Nation Builder* (New Delhi: Indian Institute of Public Administration), 2004.

Report, Indian National Congress, 1910.

Report on Indian Constitutional Reforms (Montagu-Chelmsford), paras 227-31.

Report of the United Provinces Committee on Unemployment.

Report of the Federal Structure and Minorities Committees Proceedings of the RTC, Second Session.

Rogin, Leo, *The Meaning and Validity of Economic Theory* (New York: Harper and Bros.), 1956.

Rushbrook, Williams, C. F., in Mss. Eur. R & T. 130, recorded June and August 1976, British Library Oriental and India Office Collections (OIOC).

Sapru-Jayakar Correspondence, *Sapru Papers* deposited in the Government of India, National Library (Calcutta: Belvedere), 2 series.

Sapru Papers, J 68, February 27, 1931.

Sapru Papers, H 194, March 19, 1933.

Sapru Papers, H 229, May 10, 1933.

Sapru's Speech at Agra College on 25 February 1934, reprinted in *Agra College Magazine*, Vol. IX, No. 3, April 1934.

Sapru's Presidential Address, First United Provinces of Agra and Oudh Lawyers' Conference, Allahabad, 6-7 November 1938.

Sapru, T.S., *The Indian Constitution: A Note on Its Working* (Madras: Adyar), 1926.

Savarkar, V.D., *The Indian War of Independence 1847* (New Delhi: Phoenix), 1947.

Saxena, Abha, *Indian National Movement and Liberals* (Allahabad: Chugh Publications), 1986.

Schumpeter, J.A., *History of Economic Analysis* (New York: Oxford University Press), 1954.

Sen, Sunanda, *Colonies and the Empire India, 1890-1914* (Hyderabad: Orient Longman), 1922.

Setalvad, C.H., *Recollections and Reflections* (Bombay: Padama), 1946.

Shankar, Ramahari, *Gandhi's Encounter with Indian Revolutionaries* (New Delhi: Siddharth Publications), 1996.

Sharma, Jai Narain, *Power, Politics & Corruption: A Gandhian Solution* (New Delhi: Deep and Deep), 2004.

Sharma Rashmi (ed.), *Sonia* versus *Vajpayee* (New Delhi: Deep and Deep), 2004.

Shraddhanand, Swami, *Inside Congress* (Bombay: Phoenix), 1946.

Shukla, B.D., *History of the Indian Liberal Party* (Calcutta: Bharti Publishers), 1957.

Sir R.P. Paranjpye to Justice P.N. Sapru (from a letter of condolence), Poona, January 21, 1949.

Sitaramayya, P., *History of the Congress, 1885 to 1936* (Bombay: Padama Publications), 1948.

Sitaramayya, Pattabhi, *History of Indian National Congress* (Delhi: S. Chand & Co.), 1969.

Speech, Allahabad High Court Centenary Commemoration, Vol. II.

Studenski, Paul, *The Income of Nations* (New York: New York University Press), 1958.

Syed Mahmood as Judge. Tej Bahadur Sapru, *Hindustan Review*, May 1903.

T.B. Sapru's Oral Statement before *Age of Consent Committee* made on January 16, 1929, at Allahabad.

Telegram No. 185, Mss Eur 238/25/OIOC (British Library Oriental and India Office Collections).

Tara Chand, *History of the Freedom Movement in India,* Vol. IV (New Delhi: Publications Division, Ministry of Information and Broadcasting, Government of India), 1967.

U.P. Legislative Council Proceedings, 1916.

Varma, S.N., *History of Allahabad High Court Bar Association*, Allahabad H.C. Centenary Commemoration, Vol. I.

Varma, V.P., *Modern Indian Political Thought* (Agra: Luxmi Narain Agarwal), 1961.

Walport, Stanley, *Jinnah of Pakistan* (New Delhi: Oxford University Press), 1965.

Walport, Stanley, *Tilak & Gokhale* (Bombay: University of California Press), 1962.

White Papers, para 202.

Williams, Rushbrook (ed.), *Great Men of India*, Home Library Club, 1940.

Williams Rushbrook, L.F., *India in the Years 1917-18* (Gladwin: Francis), 1975.

Wilsaon, F.W., *The Indian Chaos* (London: London Press), 1932.

Index